D0377653

Arlo & Alice & Anglicans

THE LIVES OF A NEW ENGLAND CHURCH

Also by Laura Lee

Invited to Sound
The Name's Familiar
Bad Predictions

Other Titles from Berkshire House publishers

GREAT DESTINATIONS™ *Berkshire Book: A Complete Guide*
Lauren R. Stevens

The Berkshire Reader: Writings from New England's Secluded Paradise
Edited by Richard Nunley / Drawings by Michael McCurdy

The Pioneer Valley Reader: Prose and Poetry from New England's Heartland
James C. O'Connell, Editor / Ruth Owen Jones, Picture Researcher
Foreword by Richard Todd

The New Red Lion Inn Cookbook
Suzi Forbes Chase

Muses in Arcadia: Cultural Life in the Berkshires
Timothy Cahill, Mae G. Banner, Richard Nunley, Fred Sokol

Hikes & Walks in the Berkshire Hills
Lauren R. Stevens

A Guide to Natural Places in the Berkshires
René Laubach

The Berkshires
Bill Binzen

Laura Lee

Laura Lee began her writing career at the age of 12, when she published an article called "My First Day of Junior High School." She went on to write and perform professionally with the Vorpmi comedy troupe and to earn a theater degree from Oakland University.

Before settling into a career in radio, Lee held what she calls "a number of very odd jobs." She is one of the few writers in America who was once gainfully employed as a mime.

She next worked as a radio announcer and commercial copywriter at stations in several states. It was through this career that she became familiar with Arlo Guthrie's "Alice's Restaurant."

Now a full-time writer, Lee lives in Stephentown, New York – "The Only Stephentown on Earth" – where she makes her living writing speeches and magazine articles. Her writing has appeared in such publications as *Preservation*, *Air and Space*, *Smithsonian*, and *Seattle* magazine. She is also a regular contributor to the *Times-Union* in Albany. *Arlo, Alice & Anglicans* is her third book.

Arlo & Alice & Anglicans

THE LIVES OF A NEW ENGLAND CHURCH

LAURA LEE

Berkshire House Publishers
Lee, Massachusetts

Grateful acknowledgment is made for permission to reprint excerpts from the following:
"ALICE'S RESTAURANT" by Arlo Guthrie
© Copyright 1966, 1967 (renewed) by APPLESEED MUSIC INC.
All Rights Reserved. Used by Permission.

"THE MOTORCYCLE SONG" by Arlo Guthrie
© Copyright 1967, 1969 (renewed) by APPLESEED MUSIC INC.
All Rights Reserved. Used by Permission.

The Book of Offices, © 1960 Church Pension Fund, used by Permission.

Woody Guthrie: A Life, by Joe Klein. Reprinted by permission of Alfred A. Knopf, Inc.

Rolling Blunder Review, © Arlo Guthrie, published by Rising Son Records.

ARLO, ALICE & ANGLICANS: THE LIVES OF A NEW ENGLAND CHURCH. Copyright © 2000 by Berkshire House Publishers. All rights reserved. No part of this publication may be reproduced, stored in a retrieval system, or transmitted, in any form or by any means – electronic, mechanical, photocopying, recording, or otherwise – without the prior permission in writing of the publisher and the copyright holder.

Library of Congress Cataloging-in-Publication Information.

Lee, Laura, 1969-
Arlo, Alice & Anglicans : the lives of a New England church / Laura Lee.
     p.   cm.
 Includes bibliographical references and index.
 ISBN 1-58157-010-4
1. Trinity Church (Great Barrington, Mass.)—History. 2. Great Barrington (Mass.)—Biography. 3. Great Barrington (Mass.)—History. 4. Great Barrington (Mass.)—Buildings, structures, etc. 5. Guthrie, Arlo—Homes and haunts. I. Title. II. Title: Arlo, Alice and Anglicans.
F74.G8 L44   2000
974.4'1 21—dc21   99-041883
                                                          CIP

ISBN: 1-58157-010-4

Editor: Elizabeth Tinsley
Cover, book design, and typesetting: Jane McWhorter, Blue Sky Productions
Index: Diane Brenner
Cover photograph: Michael Lavin Flower

Berkshire House books are available at substantial discounts for bulk purchases by corporations and other organizations for promotions and premiums. Special personalized editions can also be produced in large quantities. For more information, contact:

Berkshire House Publishers
480 Pleasant St., Suite 5, Lee, MA 01238
800-321-8526
E-mail: info@berkshirehouse.com
Website: www.berkshirehouse.com

Printed in the United States of America
10 9 8 7 6 5 4 3 2 1

Contents

Acknowledgments

My thanks go to the following people and organizations, without whose help this book would not have been completed.

First to my editor, Elizabeth Tinsley, whose keen suggestions and ability to deal with authors' egos made this book much better than its original.

Also thanks to everyone at Berkshire House – Jean Rousseau, Carol Bosco Baumann, Philip Rich, and Mary Osak. Without their knowledge of the community and active support of this project, this would not have been the same book.

Thanks to Maureen Maronne and the staff of the historical room of the Berkshire Athenaeum in Pittsfield, Barbara Allen of the Stockbridge Library's Historical Room, and the staff of the Mason Library in Great Barrington, and Dawn Barbieri at the Ramsdell Library in Housatonic. To Lisa Guthrie at the Guthrie Center, historians Bernard Drew and James Parrish, Pam Drum, Reverend Pierce Middleton, Roland Ginzel, Ellen Lanyon, Rachel Fletcher, Suzanne Florence, Bill and Diana Harwood, Amy Feld, Susan Grey at St. James Church, the Episcopal Diocese of Western Massachusetts, and everyone who had the time to talk to me about the church and its communities.

Special thanks to Mary Sachs, Rick Robbins, Alice Brock, and Paul Kleinwald, who have been especially helpful and generous with their time, sharing their memories and/or personal photographs for this project.

Thanks also to my family for their constant support and encouragement and for listening to me talk about a church in western Massachusetts for months on end. My father for introducing me to the publishing world. Alan Abbey and James Denn, formerly of the *Times Union*, who helped me a great deal in my development as a writer; the staff of the *Rensselaer Times Union* who taught me just how much writing I could do in a day; one of the most creative people I know, Rick Carver, whose enthusiastic support of my first attempt at play writing helped convince me I was more of a writer than an actor. Thank you to Mark Oswin, whose inventive comedy writing I have long admired, for providing just the right words of encouragement when the release of this book was delayed. Carolyn Palmer, who has provided me with an almost daily sounding board, expressing genuine joy when things go well, and heartfelt commiseration when things do not. Jennifer Hunter for being there in general. Lynda Pringle and Will Hoppey at Bag O' Cats Music – "Everybody needs a place to find some peace of mind." Tammy Pethtel for years of encouragement and enthusiasm. Valorie Howard and Tracy Utech for the same reason. John and Eileen Longo for constructing The Writers' Loft, Matt and Jodi Bergman, who wanted to be in the dedication; whoever invented microfilm, and Arlo Guthrie for writing a song so catchy I have not been able to stop humming it throughout this project – *Thanks a lot, Arlo!*

This book is dedicated to Eveline Burgert, the unnamed parishioners of the old Trinity Church, and to the iron workers, farmers, and families of the village of Van Deusenville.

THE LIVES OF A NEW ENGLAND CHURCH

"If there's a book you really want to read but it hasn't been written yet, then you must write it."

—Toni Morrison

Introduction

When I first saw the movie *Alice's Restaurant*, I was struck by two scenes. The first was set at an old white church with peeling paint. Standing outside were Alice and Ray Brock, impatiently waiting to take possession of what was to be their new home while a deconsecration ceremony was taking place inside.

There were only a handful of church members present to hear the ceremony. The camera cut briefly to an old woman seated near the middle, perhaps in her regular pew. Although she was on the screen for only seconds, her expression spoke volumes. For her, the ceremony was a funeral. She was paying her last respects to a friend that was passing from her life.

Had her great-grandparents been there when they laid the cornerstone of the building? Had her grandmother perhaps been honored with the plaque that, in a later scene, the character Shelly used as the backstop for a softball? Had she herself met her husband at a church social when she was a young redhead and fond of dancing? Had she been married at that altar? Had her children been baptized there? The questions never left me.

1

The second thing that caught my attention in the film was the fact that the song's famous "twenty-seven eight-by-ten color glossy photos" were in black and white. This entertaining discrepancy led me to wonder how much the film — and the song, for that matter — differed from reality.

Since I started working on this project, a number of people have asked, "Why did you decide to write about this church?" The answer, as best as I could phrase it, was usually "I don't know." Something about the old New England church with its curious modern history just captured my imagination. I had hoped that someone else would write a book about its history, which I could simply read. Unfortunately, no one stepped forward. If I wanted to read it, I was going to have to write it myself.

I was not raised in the Berkshires in the shadow of the Trinity Church. I am not an Episcopalian or a student of architecture. I am not even a member of the Woodstock generation. I was, in fact, born three days after a dazzled young folksinger stood on a stage at Yasgur's farm and shouted, "The New York State Thruway is closed, man!" Nor were my parents part of that long-haired, bead-wearing demographic boom. The record player of my childhood home played "At the Hop," not "Alice's Restaurant."

I must have heard "Alice's Restaurant" at some point in my child-hood, though, because when I was an intern at an alternative rock station, the music director, who was extremely knowledgeable about music released after 1985, asked me who Arlo Guthrie was and I heard myself reply, "You know . . . 'Alice's Restaurant.'" I wasn't sure why I knew that myself. The station, which played music by bands like Nirvana, Shriekback, and Toad the Wet Sprocket, mysteriously decided to do an interview with Arlo Guthrie. The music director began his interview with "Of course everyone knows about Alice's Restaurant . . ." Everything he knew about Arlo Guthrie had come directly from me. I don't remember the substance of the interview — something about buying an old church in Massachusetts, perhaps. What I do remember is that the personable musician interested me enough that I rented the movie and subsequently bought the album. I fell in love with the eighteen-minute song about two decades later than everyone else.

Not long after, I got my own air shift at "your light-rock, more-mu-sic-station, KJF" in Cadillac, Michigan. At the time, the station's format was AC/Gold, which meant that it played a combination of the innocuous hits of the day and a generous helping of oldies. I worked at KJF at the end of an era. My coworkers and I actually cued up records. For those too young to remember, the word "record" is short for "recording." It refers to black vinyl discs with grooved surfaces. Cuing a record involved putting the stylus in the groove, finding the very beginning of the sound, and then spinning the record back a quarter turn, thus allowing the turntable to get up to speed before the music began.

Cuing records didn't allow a DJ a lot of time to sit around. Today, with automation technology, DJs are largely unnecessary; the music is usually played by a computer. If you hear the announcer say, "We'll be back after this twenty-minute music marathon," that actually means that, if there's a live announcer in the booth at all, she's going to step out and let a computer play the music while she does other things. Back in the vinyl-cuing days, this was not the case. While one song played, an announcer was busy selecting the next record, cuing it up on the turntable, and retrieving the commercials, which were all recorded on individual cartridge tapes.

When I say "selecting the next record," I don't simply mean taking it out of its jacket. In those days, the music was not chosen with the aid of a computer program. Disc jockeys actually had some say in what they put on the air. The station manager did have a way of making sure we didn't play the same songs over and over. We had what was called a clock hour — a pie chart representing an hour and divided into three-minute intervals. Each interval was given a color representing a category of music we were to play in that time. The title of every song we played was written on the top of an index card. Whenever we played that song, we wrote the date and time on the card. We had to play music from the correct category at the correct time. As long as two other air shifts had played a particular song since you had, you could play it again.

This method allowed DJs to do theme shows, take requests . . . and go to the bathroom. In every radio station I've ever been in, the bathroom is about as far as humanly possible from the air studio. Therefore, when nature called, a DJ either had to be very quick or had to play a very long song. If you ask a DJ who worked at a rock station in the 1970s or early '80s, he can probably tell you from memory the exact lengths of the long songs. The longest song on our official play list was Don McLean's "American Pie" at a wonderful, get-a-snack 8:28. It was always the background music for studio emergencies. At KJF we were always getting in trouble for playing certain songs more frequently than others. Our station manager believed we all loved Chicago's "Beginnings" (7:41, with a full one-minute drum fade at the end), the Beatles' "Hey Jude" (7:02), and Al Stewart's "The Year of the Cat" (7:38). They weren't really our favorite songs; we just had to go to the bathroom, and those Dave Clark Five songs (1:51) were useless.

In the 1970s, long songs were very popular. I believe this was the bathroom phenomenon at work. After releasing a 6:26 song, a band would suddenly get lots of airplay. When MTV came on the scene in the 1980s, veejays didn't actually stand around and play the videos. They had all the time they needed to go to the bathroom, so short songs came back into style.

Of course, it was possible for an artist to carry the long thing a little too far. Even in the vinyl-disc days of radio it was difficult to drop in a song that was the length of the average sitcom. Such was the case with "Alice's Restaurant." Our station manager refused to have a copy of the 18:20 record on the premises. It would have gotten what they call "saturation play" late at night while overnight DJs (another casualty of automation) took naps. In fact, an entire mythology arose among DJs surrounding that song. Many announcers told colorful stories of things they had done during those eighteen minutes (most of them probably lies).

Despite its enduring popularity, "Alice's Restaurant" was never a chart hit. Apparently the record company couldn't figure out how to release an eighteen-minute song on a radio-friendly 45 without having it fall off the edges of the disc. (An abbreviated version, "Alice's Rock 'n' Roll Restaurant," made it to number ninety-seven on the charts.) Once a year at Thanksgiving, though, KJF listeners wanted to hear nothing else. The story that Arlo Guthrie tells in "Alice's Restaurant" begins on Thanksgiving. It is a tenuous connection to the holiday at best; the song has about as much to do with Thanksgiving as it has to do with, well, Alice. But as the marketing people would say, Arlo found a niche that was not being served. Can you name another rock and roll Thanksgiving song? Can you name another Thanksgiving song, period? That was why, once a year, members of the baby boom generation called KJF to request it.

Of course, the phenomenon is not limited to one generation. Many people my age view the '60s with the kind of nostalgia that only those who weren't there could feel. Our collective culture paints the era as a time of unbridled idealism, colorful dress, and spirited music. The everyday getting-through-life stuff has been edited out of our '60s stories. The view we have inherited is that the decade was one long demonstration march, with funny-smelling smoke, flowers, hand-holding, and great music parading straight to Woodstock.

Whether or not this was true, the spirit of the times was definitely different. In 1969 Arlo Guthrie told a *Newsweek* reporter, "All political systems are on the way out. We're finally gonna get to the point where there's no more bigotry or greed or war. Peace is the way . . . In twenty years all that stuff will be over. People are simply gonna learn that they can get more from being groovy than being greedy."

The countercultural types of my generation would not have said such a thing — and not because of the word "groovy." Like their predecessors, many of the young people who came of age in "the big '80s" were disillusioned with the Establishment (some of whose members were former hippies), but they did not believe they had the power to create a Utopia in its place. If the largest generation of young people the country had ever seen couldn't do it, what chance did they have? But many were still attracted to the symbols of that special brand of idealism: Grateful Dead tours, tie-dyed clothes, peace symbols, and the church from *Alice's Restaurant*. (Perhaps the upcoming generation, the children of the baby boomers, by virtue of their great numbers, will have the idealistic feeling that *they* can change the course of history.)

The downside of the '60s generation's anti-Establishment, "don't trust anyone over thirty" view was that it had little respect for history. The flower children were interested in writing their own histories, not reading someone else's. Some of the former members of Trinity Church were so shocked by its transformation — from a place of traditional worship with Episcopalian ritual to a hangout for hippies — that the bishop for the region created a new policy: In the future, if a church had to be deconsecrated, it would be torn down so that it might never be used for purposes that, in the words of the Reverend Pierce Middleton, "might be distasteful to the faithful."

On the other hand, had it not been for the surprising popularity of "Alice's Restaurant" and the subsequent movie, Trinity Church might have been forgotten entirely except by a few diligent historians. The building itself might well have crumbled after years of neglect. Not a lot has been written about the church and its community. It was built as a "chapel of ease" of the St. James Parish in Great Barrington--a "subchurch" for people who didn't want to travel far from their homes. In histories of the churches in the region, it appears--if it appears at all--almost as an afterthought: "There was also Trinity Church."

Even as an Episcopalian chapel of ease, Trinity Church was a symbol of forward-looking idealism. The present structure was built in 1866, just after the end of the Civil War. The Industrial Revolution was in full swing. Now that resources did not have to be allocated to the war effort, modern inventions like steam engines, steamboats, gas lighting, and the telegraph were making the world seem smaller. It was an exciting time to be alive. The area known as Van Deusenville, Massachusetts, was growing and thriving. The parishioners decided to tear down the existing small stone church and build a structure that would accommodate the growth that was sure to come.

But the town didn't boom in the way the people expected. The iron furnace that employed most of the men closed in 1897. One by one the shops closed, and people moved away. The church fell into a slow decline. Regular services continued there until 1947, the year Arlo Guthrie was born. After that they were held irregularly until what was left of the congregation finally sold the building in 1962.

Trinity Church is a fossil of this abandoned dream for a community — a community that never was, and never would be, the subject of a movie. On the surface it may seem that an Episcopal congregation in the Berkshires of the late 1800s would have little in common with the rebellious youths in *Alice's Restaurant*. Yet, in a way, they are very much the same. Each group had its dream of the future, a dream that, for a time, brought people together. They gathered at the same church building. They sang songs and told stories that spoke of their common views. Together they celebrated their victories, mourned their friends' passing, and leaned on one another in times of trouble. Then, all too suddenly, times changed; the communities disbanded; the building became an empty shell waiting for a new community to give it new life. This is what draws me to the building: There are few churches that have had so many distinct and fascinating rebirths.

History is an inexact science. It relies on the faulty memories of human beings, who are endowed by their creator with the creative desire to tell a good story. Arlo Guthrie, in fact, gave me the following advice on writing this book: "No one is a reliable source. Don't believe anybody." "Facts" are recalled and recorded by human beings. One person's set of facts does not always correspond with another's. With many retellings, it is easy for details to become muddled. For example, it has been widely — and erroneously — reported that the wooden structure of Trinity Church burned to the ground in 1896 and was rebuilt. In fact, it was St. James, the parent church in Great Barrington, that burned that year in "the great Railroad Street fire" that destroyed twenty-two buildings.

In telling the story of the Van Deusenville church — its construction, its period of prosperity, its decline — I relied on church records, newspaper archives, old photographs, memories of neighbors, and a small amount of extrapolation based on what later tenants discovered about the property. For the more modern history, I relied on personal interviews and newspaper and magazine clippings.

No history will ever be able to capture what it was really like to be in the building — the smells, the sounds, the tiny details and little moments lost forever in time. I hope, however, that I have in some small way expressed some of the spirit that makes the church so interesting to me. The building has provided the background for important moments for many people — as Trinity Church, as "Alice's Church," as the Guthrie Center. It holds a special place in many people's hearts.

In 1992 Arlo Guthrie used all his savings and "mortgaged everything" to buy the building that had played such an important role in his life. I hope that this book will capture a little bit of the feeling that made it a landmark he felt compelled, once again, to call his own.

JUDY BEISLER

"You may have heard this one
before . . . I know I have."

— Arlo Guthrie
"Alice's Restaurant:
The Massacree Revisited"

Housatonic, July 5, 1995

The designers of the 124-year-old pine and chestnut church on Division Street in the Housatonic village of the city of Great Barrington, Massachusetts, certainly did not have a recording studio in mind. The building stands only a few feet from an active railroad track, and each car of a passing train causes the walls to click and clack to its rhythm.

On this particular evening, the church was not even much to look at. Its formerly white walls were now a beige showcase of peeling paint. Most of the stained glass had been replaced with ordinary clear stuff years earlier. The roof leaked, and the bell tower was a buzzing home for bees.

Yet for musician Arlo Guthrie, there could be no better place to record--at least this particular song. Five years earlier, Arlo had told a reporter that when the time and place were right he would record an updated version of his most famous musical tale, "The Alice's Restaurant Massacree."

9

"It's just a matter of getting the right recording of the right timing of the right audience on the right night," he said.

Tonight was the right night. The timing would be right. It couldn't have been better, in fact. Because after all these years, Arlo was the owner of the place where it had all happened--the "scene of the crime." Thirty years before, he had been one of many young people to attend an unconventional Thanksgiving dinner in this building, which was then the home of his friends and former teachers Ray and Alice Brock. He and another friend, Rick Robbins, offered to take out the garbage. If the town dump had not been closed that Thanksgiving Day, the youths would not have disposed of the waste by dumping it down the side of a hill. They would not have been arrested for the crime, and Arlo would never have written a humorous eighteen-minute song about how his arrest for littering affected his chances of being sent to Vietnam.

But the dump was closed, and "Alice's Restaurant" was written. The song not only launched Arlo's career but also made him a celebrity, and he brought his fame right back to the church. When director Arthur Penn decided to use the famous song as the basis for a movie, he shot it largely in and around this building, using many of the actual participants in the song's events as actors.

So it's not hard to understand why, when Arlo had the opportunity to buy the church years later, he had to do it — whether he could afford to or not. He's not the only one who feels this way about the place. The church was filled to capacity on that July evening, as it had been in its heyday as an Episcopalian sanctuary. The spectators were sitting, not in pews, but in gray metal folding chairs arranged in neat rows. They wore name tags outlined with the words MA'S HANUMAN GAR and THE GUTHRIE

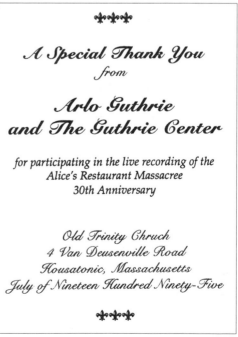

A Special Thank You
from

Arlo Guthrie
and The Guthrie Center

for participating in the live recording of the
Alice's Restaurant Massacree
30th Anniversary

Old Trinity Chruch
4 Van Deusenville Road
Housatonic, Massachusetts
July of Nineteen Hundred Ninety-Five

CENTER. Some of them had come from miles away.

Deb Denucci and her husband, Mark, drove from Binghamton, New York, to be there, and planned to drive straight back when the event was over. "Seven hours of driving for a twenty-minute song," she said with a laugh.

They didn't mind the drive, and they were happy to sit on that warm evening in a crowded room with the windows closed, listening to a story they'd heard hundreds of times before — because the combination of singer, song, and setting was magical. That day the audience would be right.

Arlo looked out at the group gathered in his church, and his fingers plucked out the chord progression he could probably strum in his sleep. "You may have heard this song before," he began with a roll of his eyes. "I know I have . . ."

As he played, he could not help but think about days gone by and the people who had come in and out of the church over the years . . .

"Having all that room where the pews used to be . . ."

— Arlo Guthrie
"Alice's Restaurant"

Great Barrington, 1962

A s the sun rises in the east, it shines through the brightly colored arched windows of what was once a church. A rainbow is cast into the cavernous interior, revealing a room full of . . . rooting swine. Difficult to picture? It was for Pierce Middleton, the new rector of the St. James Parish in Great Barrington, Massachusetts.

Dr. Middleton came to St. James on January 1, 1961. Besides being an Episcopal priest, he held an M.A. in medieval history and prehistoric archaeology from the University of Edinburgh and an M.A. and Ph.D. in Early American History from Harvard. St. James Church was Trinity Church's parent congregation. As the rector of the parish, the neglected Housatonic church was his responsibility. The building was boarded up now, the paint was peeling, the lawn was unkempt, and weeds grew up against the walls. No services had been held in the church for years, but as long as the parish owned it, it had to pay for insurance to maintain the property. It was getting more expensive even to clean, as the regular cleaning woman had upped her price from $10 to $15 a visit:

> To Trinity Church,
> For cleaning church $15. Due to condition of church, I had to spend extra time on cleaning. Also includes a helper.
> Respectfully,
> Pauline Roberts

When two boys snuck into the building on a lark and broke some of the blue and violet stained-glass windows with a rock, it became clear that the St. James Parish could no longer ignore the problem of what to do with the old Trinity Church. The vestry took a vote and decided it was time to sell.

"They continued for as long as they could," Dr. Middleton says. "It was costing us just to maintain it. There was hardly anything we could do."

The boys, incidentally, were found guilty of vandalism, and the judge ordered them to make restitution. They would work and pay the church a portion of their salaries each month until the cost of the destroyed windows was recouped. Since the windows were not to be replaced by the church, the bishop put the money in escrow to be used for the boys' education when they were old enough to go to college.

Because Reverend Middleton had a reverence for history, he was not inclined to sell the church to just anyone. He hoped that it might be used by another religious order. A Greek Orthodox church expressed some interest. Representatives of the church came out to look at the building. They were pleased with the structure, but they wanted more acreage than the Trinity yard provided.

So an ad was placed in the *Berkshire Eagle:*

> Church Building FOR SALE
> Formerly Trinity Church . . . Located in Van Deusenville
> A large building with some contents.
> About an acre of land.
> Complete $2,000
> Contact—R. K. WHEELER, Great Barrington
> TELEPHONE ONE

(Allowing for inflation, $2,000 is the equivalent of roughly $10,000 today.)

Telephone One did not ring off the hook. A cavernous A-frame that was prohibitively expensive to heat, had no plumbing or bedrooms and little electricity, and looked like a church would appeal only to a very special buyer. Finally one call came in, from a local farmer. He thought the structure would make a splendid barn for his livestock. He could store his hay in the bell tower and let the hogs roam the sanctuary. With its exposed beams and spare construction, the sanctuary did, in an odd way, resemble a barn. But, even though the building would be deconsecrated before it was sold, Reverend Middleton was not prepared to put pigs in the place, and he turned the farmer down.

Then a second offer came, from a woman named Mary Pelkey, of Lenox. She was a real estate broker and the registrar at the Stockbridge School, a private boarding school in nearby Interlaken.

"I was buying old houses, offbeat properties like barns, carriage houses, one-room schoolhouses, a sawmill, abandoned farms," she says. "It was not a time when such things were in demand. They were all waiting for someone like me to come along. And I learned by trial and error to restore them and improve them Before you knew it they were in demand, and I would sell one, buy another. And so it went."

But the abandoned church was more than an offbeat property or an investment for Mary Pelkey. It had sentimental value as well. It had been a regular stop on family vacations and was a favorite of her daughters, Zina and Alice.

"My father grew up in Pittsfield," Alice recalls. "He had family there. We lived in Brooklyn, and we used to drive up to the Berkshires to visit family. We would stop and stay overnight with Grandma and other relatives. He had an unusual route he'd take out of New York. He liked to stop and have lunch in a funny little town that had a wonderful general store. So we always took this kind of route. We always made up stories about places. One of the places we stopped was that church. It was never open. We just used to stop there and walk around. I used to say, 'When I grow up, I'm going to live here.'"

As Mary remembers the trips, the girls amused themselves in the back of the Chevy wagon by pretending to own all the landmarks they passed. "The George Washington Bridge was a biggie. They fought over that for ages. The old church in Van Deusenville couldn't be resolved that easily. They both wanted it. So we changed our route and didn't drive past it anymore. The year we moved to the Berkshires and weren't traveling anymore, I snuck out by myself to look at the neglected church, and one day there was a sign on it — 'For Sale.' Of course I bought the Van Deusenville church."

She was sure that the building would appeal to her daughter, Alice, and son-in-law, Ray Brock. Alice and Ray were also working at the Stockbridge School. Although she worked as a librarian, Alice was an artist who put her creative stamp on everything she did, from painting to decorating to cooking. Ray, who worked as a shop teacher, was a trained architect and sculptor with boundless energy and a vividly creative mind. A pair of self-described beatniks, Alice and Ray were not likely to be happy in a suburban split-level, but an old Gothic church that they could transform into their own kind of home was irresistible.

"We'd put in one year at Stockbridge School, and my mother knew I wanted to get back to New York," Alice says. "So she knew she could lure Ray to this church. I'm not saying all this consciously went through her mind."

The Brocks brought over three or four friends, including students from the Stockbridge School, to get their opinions on the church before they made the final decision to buy it. It was run down, dusty, full of junk, and needed painting, but the old foot pump organ was still there. So was some of the spiritual magic. Everyone agreed it was a great place. The church had found its buyers.

Mary Pelkey told a *Berkshire Eagle* reporter that her daughter and son-in-law would use the church as a studio and a summer and week-end retreat from the city — something Alice says she probably made up to make them sound "respectable and not like the freaks we were." She also assured the reporter that the studio would be a private studio only — there would be nothing commercial about it.

Before the Brocks could take possession of the property, however, a number of things had to be done. Many of the church fixtures had already been removed. Most of the books and linens were given to a new mission that had been built near an Air Force base, although some remained. Alice still has a few. Members of the mission also came and took as many of the chestnut pews as they could fit into a truck, leaving about twelve behind.

Trinity also had a set of Communion silver, a gift from St. James Church. When Trinity was sold, the silver was donated to the bishop of Haiti to be used in rural churches in that country. Dr. Middleton did keep one piece, a flagon for pouring the wine for the Eucharist. Because the silver probably dated back to the eighteenth century, in years to come he would place it on the St. James altar at Easter and Christmas as a reminder of the past. Other historic reminders were the memorial plaques on the walls of the church. Plans were made to remove them and take them to St. James, where future family members could view them, but this apparently never happened. Two worn and slightly paint-spattered memorial plaques remain on the wall to this day. The first is to the memory of John H. Coffing, who was instrumental in the building of the church and of the village of Van Deusenville (and about whom there will be more later). The second plaque reads:

> In memory of Eveline Stone Burgert
> Wife of Garrett Burgert
> Born May 25, 1827 — Died April 21, 1903
> Faithful Unto Death

Years later, the movie *Alice's Restaurant* would feature a scene in which the character Shelly, newly released from drug rehabilitation, comes to stay with Ray and Alice at the church. As he tries to quell his urge to shoot up, he paces nervously, briefly stopping to look at Eveline's memorial plaque. After staring at it for a moment, he hurls a softball at it. In her analysis of the film, Robin Wood describes the character as "impotently trying to smash it and what it stands for. It stands, in fact, for two things: the sense of stable family relationships as well as a memento mori . . . Shelly dies because life — both his inner life and the life around him — offers him no stability."

Of course the plaque had not been placed on the wall for the film. It was a memorial to a very active member of the church community, Eveline A. Burgert, the youngest of the four children of Lydia and Eber Stone. Eber Stone built the second home in Housatonic. He made spinning wheels for a living, first by hand in a shop near his house. In 1818 his father, Captain Ezekial Stone, gave him a plot of land on which he built a shop for the manufacture of wheels. Eber Stone was active in founding

17

Trinity Church and was one of its original two wardens. Eveline lived in Housatonic until she married the widower Garrett Burgert in 1871. He owned a large plot of land around the corner from the church, on what is now Route 41. Garrett's first wife was Electra Van Deusen, the daughter of Isaac Van Deusen, who was also instrumental in the formation of the church (and about whom there will also be more later). When Eveline died in 1903, the *Berkshire Courier* ran the following obituary:

> Mrs. Burgert was from her girlhood a member of Trinity Church, Van Deusenville, and for many years, particularly during her residence there, she was closely identified with that church and devoted much of her time to the interest of the church and Sunday school. She loved the Holy Place and was always happy in her labors for its welfare. Her life was one of loving service and constant devotion to her family and friends. No unkind criticism of others was ever spoken by her. We who have known something of the sincerity of her Christian character will long cherish her memory, and are grateful that we have so often witnessed and experienced the genuineness of her love.

On April 10, 1963, Robert K. Wheeler, senior warden of the St. James Parish, described in a letter to Lincoln Cain, the attorney for Mary Pelkey, some last-minute details that would need to be hammered out before the church property could change hands.

> Your client, Mrs. Pelkey, may already have contacted you concerning her desire to purchase the Trinity Church property at Van Deusenville, which, as you know, is part of Great Barrington. The sale price is $2,000, of which $200 is to be paid at this time and the balance on the passing of the title. Purchase to include pews, organ, carpet and books now on the premises.
>
> I have definitely ascertained that the water company water line is directly in front of the property on Division Street B, also that, as far as I can ascertain, if the building is used as residence and studio, there will be no conflict with any zoning

ordinance. $3000 fire insurance now on the property to be trans-
ferred at time of sale or present insurance policy re-written.

A mere detail, but the church must be deconsecrated first
by Bishop Hatch and this action has already been requested . . .

The deconsecration of a church is a fairly rare event, but common
enough to merit a prescribed ceremony in the *Book of Offices* (now it is
listed in the *Book of Occasional Services*). "It's very rare. It would only
happen once in the lifetime of a building," says the Reverend Cannon
Robert S. S. Whitman, who performed the ceremony. It is the only
deconsecration he has ever performed. Only a dozen or so people witnessed the ceremony on June 17, 1963. Alice and Ray Brock were asked
not to attend.

"I think the parishioners probably went through all the sorrow before the ceremony happened," Reverend Whitman says. "I'm sure there
were people who were sad to see it go, but no fuss was made."

As the rector of St. James, Pierce Middleton was in attendance, but,
unlike in the movie, he did not perform the service. After the few parishioners settled quietly in their familiar pews, the service began:

Good people, you know already the reasons for which it
is thought well that this building, hitherto consecrated and
separated from all worldly uses, shall be no longer continued in this use, but shall be taken down or appointed for
other purposes. To many of you, this building has become
endeared by many sacred memories, and you will suffer a
loss and feel that something has passed out of your lives.
Such persons will be comforted by the assurance that the
Presence of God, and the consolation of our holy religion,
are not tied to any one place or building. We have caused that
the Altar hitherto in this church should be carefully removed
and protected from desecration. And this fabric, accordingly, is
thereby forever secularized, and the Sentence of Consecration,
heretofore pronounced by our Right Reverend predecessor,
is revoked and canonically annulled, and this place, heretofore a holy place and sacred to the preaching of God's holy
Word, and the ministration of His holy sacraments, is hereby

pronounced secular and unconsecrated, and no longer within our canonical jurisdiction. Amen.

After they had finished speaking, the priests put on their hats to symbolically show that they were no longer standing on sacred ground.

"A solemn ceremony last week saw the venerable Trinity Church in the Van Deusenville section of Great Barrington deconsecrated," the *Berkshire Eagle* reported, "and the way cleared for a new career for the stately structure."

No one could have imagined on that day the "new career" that lay ahead for the building; that in a few years this very ceremony would be reenacted before the camera for a famous Hollywood movie director; that for years after that, curious travelers would stop to take pictures and peer into its windows. Instead, to the few in attendance, June 17, 1963, was the end of an era, the final period at the end of the history of Trinity Church.

"These churches are the costly memorials, dear to God and to man, of the tears, the toils, the sufferings of your fathers, long gathered to their rest. There is none other heritage more precious than these."

— Reverend Samuel P. Parker
First rector of Trinity Church of
Van Deusenville

Upper Sheffield, ca. 1758

Colonial New England was not a good place to be a criminal. Brutal punishments were carried out in public to serve as both deterrent and entertainment. Hangings were carnival-like affairs; food and drink were served. For noncapital offenses, whipping and branding were both common. Some who went afoul of the law were placed in the pillory, a pair of boards with holes for the hands and head, or the stocks, which held the prisoner by the ankles. Crowds gathered to hurl dirt, rocks, rotten food, and verbal abuse at their wayward neighbors. After an hour or more of this punishment, insects would often fly into the prisoners' faces, drawn by the rotten tomatoes and eggs.

Until 1758, the area now known as Great Barrington, Massachusetts, then called Upper Sheffield, had had no need for the stocks. It had been only thirty years since the area was deeded to English settlers by the

Mahicans, a tribe of the Algonquian nation. The rough terrain of the Berkshire Mountains and its distance from the ocean kept the new community in the Housatonic River valley somewhat isolated and protected from the tribulations besetting the rest of Massachusetts. But in 1758 Isaac Van Deusen and John, Peter, and Garret Burghardt committed an offense so serious a set of stocks had to be built just to confine them. Their crime? They refused to go to church.

Modern-day Great Barrington is a town of churches. The three-block stretch of the town's main street alone has four. In 1758, however, there was only one, the Puritans' Congregationalist Church. The early settlers of the area were primarily Dutch and English. The majority of the English were Puritans who had left their native country to escape religious persecution. A small minority were Anglicans, members of the officially recognized Church of England. They had not come to America to escape prejudice and persecution; most had come simply to seek their fortunes. The Dutch were mostly Lutherans, who in the beginning were content to join with the Puritan majority and build a common place of Protestant worship.

Dutch involvement was vital to the town because the Dutch were among the wealthiest and most prominent citizens of the community. Coonrod Burghardt, the father of John, Peter, and Garret, was one of the founders of the Housatonic colony, which later became known as Sheffield and finally Great Barrington. As a fur trader along a trail called the New England Path, Burghardt had many dealings with the Native Americans who lived in the hills and in 1724 purchased a large tract of land from them. In the 1750s he and Isaac "The Rich" Van Deusen were the largest landholders in western Massachusetts. (They were also in-laws. Van Deusen married Burghardt's daughter, Fiche.)

Isaac Van Deusen was described in an 1829 text, written by his (perhaps somewhat biased) grandson, as "a devout man, of unblemished character, of the strictest integrity and universally respected for his benevolence and hospitality. He was a true patriot, sober, meek, temperate, true and just in all his dealings, a venerable man, and a philanthropist." The Burghardt brothers were likewise described as being "of unblemished character."

Isaac Van Deusen was one of the seaters for the meetinghouse, which had fifteen pews, "fourteen for landed gentry with one for the minister's family." Seating order was determined by money and status. Seaters were told "to have special regard to estates, as contained in the last and present year's lists, and also to the age of particular persons, accounting each years age, above sixteen equal to £4 on the list, and also to persons honorary, whether by commission or otherwise."

Coonrod Burghardt bought "the second pew east from the south door" for £49. Isaac Van Deusen bought the "pew between the last pew and the stairs" for £35.

When the Puritans came to America, they did not envision it as a melting pot but as a place where they could establish their own religion. Their form of worship had its origins in seventeenth-century England as a reaction against the Church of England, which they felt was not sufficiently distinguishable from Catholicism. Although the Anglican Church was created by Henry VIII and broke its ties with Pope Pius V during the reign of Elizabeth I, it had made few major changes in its rituals. As the Reverend Latta Griswold wrote in *The Episcopal Church: Its Teaching and Worship*: "It is common to hear our Church sometimes grouped with the Protestants. This is true in so far as with them we protest against the claims of the Papacy, but on the other hand in our doctrine of the Church, the Sacraments, the Ministry, we are Catholic."

It was this close identification with the spirit of Catholicism that the Puritans renounced. In America they wasted no time setting up their own religious laws. Anglican worship was especially singled out for censure under these new laws. Early on in Massachusetts the Anglican *Book of Common Prayer* and the celebration of Christmas were outlawed. Only members of the Congregational Church were allowed to vote.

Anglicans throughout Massachusetts began to stand up against the laws in the early 1700s. One of the boldest protests took place at Yale College on September 13, 1722, when Yale president and Congregationalist minister Timothy Cutler and six other professors announced they were converting to the Church of England. As historian Henry May wrote: "The effect was similar to that which might have been produced in 1925 if the Yale football team had suddenly joined the Communist Party."

In the mountains of Upper Sheffield, however, such events had little effect. There it was still illegal to question church doctrines, and all residents were required to attend church at least once every three months. The minister of the Congregationalist Church, Samuel Hopkins, was hired

23

December 28, 1743, when there were only thirty families in town. He was given a salary and a hundred acres of land, called the Upper Housatonic property, which included parts of what are now Great Barrington, Stockbridge, and Lee. Hopkins's sermons must have been a shock to Anglican sensibilities. The preacher was known for impassioned rhetoric full of colorful references to sin and to "the hottest fire that can be imagined, or exist, through endless ages." The Anglicans were few in number, however, and for the most part had few complaints.

When the Dutch finally did refuse to attend services, it was not because of political ideals about the separation of church and state. Nor did the references to fire and brimstone especially bother them. Their only objection to Hopkins's long English sermons was that they could hardly understand them. When they went to Hopkins and asked for occasional services in their native language, the minister is said to have replied, "What! Dutch preaching in the meetinghouse? No, that shall never be!" Having been so involved with the early church and having contributed so much money, people like "Rich Isaac" and the Burghardt family must have felt entitled to some say in how things were run. They saw the refusal of their request as more than a denial of services in their language; it was an act of contempt. Then and there they decided to boycott the church and spend their Sundays meditating and reading their Bibles in the comfort of their own homes.

Hopkins did not take the willful desertion of some of the most prominent citizens of the town lightly. After more than three months had passed, he preached a sermon urging loyal churchmen to go to the magistrate and report the absent Dutch. They had no choice but to comply. Among the "delinquents" brought before the judge were Isaac Van Deusen and the Burghardt brothers.

The magistrate was sympathetic to their plight, but they had, after all, broken the law. He gave them a choice: They could pay a fine or be confined to the stocks. Burghardt turned to his friend, Judge Timothy Woodbridge, a respected schoolmaster of the Indians in Stockbridge, for advice. The judge counseled the group to choose the stocks, because that punishment would reflect badly on those who had ordered it.

So the first set of stocks was built in Sheffield. The dissenters were seated on a board with their ankles locked between wooden planks. But no rotten tomatoes were hurled on that day, nor pebbles, nor filth. No unkind words were spoken. This was due less to the benevolence of the spectators than to the presence of Hendrick Burghardt, who stood beside the stocks with his blunderbuss and pellet pouch and challenged the onlookers to insult his younger brothers. Judge Woodbridge was also on hand, cracking jokes and creating a lighthearted mood.

Instead of being a victory for Hopkins, the Dutchmen's act of martyrdom cost him points among members of the community. Following their punishment, the Dutchmen agreed that they would be "good men and true" and follow the letter of the law. They attended church once every three months, but no more, as required.

Hopkins was clearly displeased by the erosion of his standing in the community. One Sunday he spotted Isaac Van Deusen among the worshipers, putting in his trimonthly appearance, and it must have galled him. He pointed directly at Isaac and said, "Every Sunday you are not here, you are in Hell!"

This incident strengthened Dutch resolve to break ties with the Congregationalist Church. The high-handed treatment of the Lutherans was not lost on the other minority group in the area, the Anglicans. The two groups were soon united in their common goal of forming their own church. Over the next few years, both groups employed the services of traveling ministers to preach and baptize their children according to their own beliefs. Although they paid for these services, they were still required to attend the official church and pay £20 a year for its support.

If the prominent people who instigated the break with the Congregationalist Church were Lutherans, why didn't the Anglicans join them in *their* worship, instead of the other way around? Perhaps the Dutch wanted to get back at Hopkins and knew that an Anglican Church would be more effective in that regard. More likely, however, they became Anglicans because of the work of the Society for the Propagation of the Gospel in Foreign Parts, a missionary service begun by the Church of England. The society had been established by the Reverend Dr. Thomas Bray, a scholar, religious author, and priest who was active in prison reform, building schools for blacks in the British colonies, and aiding the poor. With its mission of advancing the cause of the Church of England throughout the world, the society built more than one hundred churches in the American colonies between 1700 and 1776. They were especially numerous in those parts of New England where Anglicanism was being actively discouraged. Anglican ministers traveled the area, unafraid of controversy.

In June 1761, Upper Sheffield became Great Barrington, named for Lord Barrington of England, a relative of the provincial governor, Sir Francis Bernard. With a new government came new rules. The Anglicans, who now had enough members to make up their own parish, petitioned to be relieved of their obligation to pay taxes to someone else's church. Samuel Hopkins, apparently tired of his struggle to keep the dissenters in his flock, said, "Whosoever does not like my doctrine may pull up stakes and be gone."

The Anglicans were now free to worship in their own fashion without fear of arrest. They enlisted the help of Thomas Davies, a missionary with the Society for the Propagation of the Gospel in Foreign Parts. Davies wrote to his English sponsors on December 18, 1762:

"A few families in Barrington, westernmost settlement in that Province, sent their earnest desire that I would come and visit them. I went and preached to a large concourse of people and baptized some children. I instructed them into the meaning and propriety of the Common Prayer Book. They informed me that many of them had long been dissatisfied with their dissenting instructions, being constantly taught rigid Calvinism."

Even so, for many years Anglicans still had to register with town authorities to be excused from attending the Congregational Church, and appear to have been the target of some continued persecution. (It would be another century before the Fourteenth Amendment to the Constitution would apply to state religious laws.)

In 1763 Davies again wrote to the society and said of the Great Barrington Anglicans: "They are made to support a dissenting teacher, equally with the dissenters themselves, and can find no release from the laws of the governments . . . and are obliged after all, to sit down under their burden to support a form of religion which they abhor."

Several months later, Davies wrote: "Just before I wrote in June, 1763, they did imprison fifteen days, two persons of as good character as any in the town; the one educated in the Church, the other a Lutheran, for no other reason but because they did not go to meeting. As to their rates of ministerial tax, which amounts to about 20 pounds sterling, per annum, that they are obliged to pay, without the least hesitation to support the dissenting teacher, although he, in almost all his sermons, casts the bitterest invectives and sarcasms against the Church of England as a Church."

In a letter dated March 14, 1764, another traveling minister, Roger Viets, reported that he was arrested for performing a marriage ceremony:

> ... In one of my visits I joined a couple in Marriage, having previously had evidence of their legal publication, of the consent of the parents and guardians of the parties, and that there was no just cause or impediment why they should not be joined together. For this I was arrested at my next visit on the 30th of January, in the midst of my congregation, and in my robes, soon after the conclusion of the morning Service, and conveyed within one or two hours to the County Jail, where I continued 8 days ... The gentleman who prosecuted me was one Mr. Mark Hopkins, town clerk, county treasurer, King's Attorney, and brother to the dissenting teacher at Great Barrington, who took me to Mr. Timothy Hopkins, brother to the same dissenting teacher. My expense in this affair, besides the disgraceful insults and indignities I have suffered, amounts to a considerable sum, and has been of great detriment to me and the people of my Mission ...

The Anglicans were not deterred, however. In 1763 John Williams, Samuel Lee, and John Burghardt formed a committee to build their own church on land Burghardt had donated. Isaac Van Deusen also contributed generously to the project. Because glass was expensive in colonial times, it was often seen as a status symbol. The new church, modeled on Christ Church in Stratford, Connecticut, had many large arched windows — so many, in fact, that it was sometimes referred to as "the glass house." The church also had the first church bell in town, a ship's bell donated by a member — "the first which summoned the villagers to the house of prayer."

The first service was held in the new building, then called Christ Church, on Christmas Day, 1764. Thomas Davies performed the service. Fourteen people participated. Davies gave a simple sermon, read from the Gospel according to St. Matthew, and baptized four children.

The church did not have a full-time minister until 1770, when Gideon Bostwick filled that role. A graduate of Yale, he was ordained at St. James Church in London. He returned to the colonies in 1770 as a missionary with the Society for the Propagation of the Gospel in Foreign Parts. Along with his duties in Great Barrington, Bostwick ministered to the people of Lanesboro, Massachusetts, and traveled to forty-seven missions from Connecticut to New Hampshire. He rode through the forest on horseback, it is said, finding his way with marked trees. In 1880 the Reverend Samuel Parker described his travels:

"While residing at Bristol, Rhode Island, he had an appointment of an Episcopal visitiation in a church some miles distant. In order to keep it, he must cross the Bristol Ferry where I remember to have seen waves higher than I ever saw them in the Atlantic. A great storm came up and made it dangerous to cross the ferry. Nothing daunted, the Bishop told the ferry-man that he must and would take the risk. The Bishop stretched himself flat on the bottom of the boat, crossed and kept his appointment."

Bostwick was described as "a faithful and pious minister, indefatigable in his labors, devout in his religious affections, humane and benevolent in his feelings, of cheerful, facetious humor, plain, courteous and affable in his manners and was much endeared to his people." In other words, he was very popular. People said that wherever he went, a church sprouted.

Had it not been for his popularity, it is possible that the church might not have survived the Revolutionary War. Ministers of the Anglican Church were all ordained in England and swore allegiance to the British Crown. Because of this, many Anglicans remained loyal to the mother country in what they saw as a civil uprising, not a war between two nations. One-third of the Anglicans in New England in 1776 returned to England or fled to Canada when the revolution began. Those who remained were viewed with great suspicion by the revolutionaries.

Many of the church's members were mentioned in a letter dated July 9, 1776, that was sent to residents who refused to sign a bill agreeing to boycott British goods. Among those named were Gideon Bostwick, various members of the Van Deusen family, including "Isaac Van Deusen, Jun'r," and members of the Burghardt family, including "Peter Burghardt ye second."

"The People of this Town are very uneasy that you have not yet resigned your arms," the letter said. "And we find they are determined to take your arms, in their own way unless you resign them of your own accord. In order to prevent further confusion and mischief we advise you to resign your arms immediately to Sergeant Joshua Root who the committee have desired to receive and take charge of the same, and we have desired him to give you Notice of this advice."

At the beginning of the war, there were twelve Anglican clergymen in Massachusetts. By the end there were only three, among them Gideon Bostwick. When the fighting was over, the fledgling church in Great Barrington was renamed St. James. Most likely it was named for the chapel in London where Bostwick had been ordained. The religion itself was also renamed, to reflect the severing of ties with England. In September 1784, a group of five clergymen met in Boston to determine what form the American version of the Church of England should take. They decided: "That the Episcopal Church in the United States of America is and ought to be independent of all foreign authority ecclesiastical and civil; That the doctrines of the Gospel be maintained as now professed by the Church of England and uniformity of worship be continued as near as may be to the Liturgy of said Church; That the succession of Ministry be agreeable to the usage which requireth three orders of Bishops, priests and Deacons."

Thus St. James Episcopal Church of Great Barrington was born. The congregation survived and thrived into the next century. Looking back on this period in the church's history on the occasion of the 1880 Episcopal Convocation held at St. James Church, Reverend Samuel P. Parker would say:

> These churches are the costly memorials, dear to God and to man, of the tears, the toils, the sufferings of your fathers, long gathered to their rest. There is none other heritage more precious than these. I have no wish to revive animosities that have died. But it is my duty to remind the convocation that the foundations of this parish were laid in suffering. St. James' church today stands the witness of the martyr-assertion of the Rights of Conscience: of the brave vindication of Religious Liberty. The persecutions which its founders endured were the faults of the age, the decedents of which have learned far better. God be praised that good will and Christian love

have taken the place of fines and of the pillory. But honor to the memory of your intrepid fathers who shrunk not from these. But while we engrave on our hearts the lesson of courage in behalf of right; let the other lesson be eternal there that the most excellent way of spreading the truth, first, midst, last, is charity towards those who are different from us.

The village of Van Deusenville was located four miles from St. James Church. Although that is no distance at all in an automobile, it was a long and hilly route by horseback or on foot. By the early 1800s, St. James had enough members in Van Deusenville to warrant the building of a "chapel of ease" to make it more convenient for those people to attend services. It was called the St. James Chapel. It would later be known as Trinity Church.

"On Williams River, half a mile from its entrance into the Housatonic, where in 1822 there were only one or two dwelling houses, a saw-mill and a grist-mill, there is now a thriving village called Van Deusenville. Here are now eighteen dwelling houses, a post office and tavern, two stores and two factories, one of cotton and the other of woolen. Here also a chapel is now building for the worship of God."

— Reverend Sylvester Burn
The History of Berkshire, 1829

Williams' Old Mills, ca. 1781

I n the early 1780s, around the time the first American Episcopal diocese — the diocese of Connecticut — was formed, Isaac Van Deusen came into possession of a large parcel of land. The property was called "Williams' Old Mills" for its previous owner, John Williams.

In 1749 John Williams had been granted "the stream, commonly called the Old Saw-Mill Brook, and land sufficient for an accommodation of setting a saw-mill and grist-mill on said stream, in case the said Williams erect and perfect said mills within the space of one year after the passing of this vote; the same to remain and to be continued to the said Williams so long as he shall keep said mills in good repair and order." He built the mills and a blacksmith's shop and kept "said mills in good repair and order" until his death in 1776.

Isaac Van Deusen maintained the property until 1787, when he was eighty-four years old. He passed away January 14, 1796, at the age of ninety-three, leaving behind six sons, Matthew, Abraham, Coonrad, John, Jacob, and Isaac. It was Jacob who inherited Williams' Mills. In turn, he willed the estate to his son, Captain Isaac L. Van Deusen. Captain Van Deusen was already a prominent citizen. He was town treasurer and represented the town in the General Court at Boston. (His son, Edwin Martin Van Deusen, went on to become an Episcopal priest and rector of Grace Church in Utica, New York.) By the time he inherited the property, the sawmill was gone, and in 1829 the gristmill burned to the ground. But the younger Isaac was determined to build a prosperous town around his land. He first built a woolen factory, then a cotton factory; both thrived. Consequently, the area was named Van Deusenville.

By 1828 Van Deusenville had, in addition to the two mills, eighteen homes, a post office, a tavern, and two shops, but if it was to be a real community, it would need something more. So, like the grandfather for whom he was named, Isaac became a prominent member of a group that wanted a church to call its own.

Around Thanksgiving 1828 (an Episcopal but not yet a national holiday), a committee was formed to study the feasibility of erecting a chapel at Van Deusenville. A rough paraphrase of their decision might be: "Sure, you can build a chapel, as long as it won't cost us anything." They then chose a group to draft a somewhat wordier report. The writers, Reverend Gilbert, Major Samuel Rosseter, General Timothy Wainwright, Isaac L. Van Deusen, Eber Stone, and Hezekiah Lathrop, submitted the proposal at the December 13th society meeting. The report stated:

> 1stly, That it shall ever and always be continued a chapel in continuation with the parent church so long as it shall stand or in consequence it shall ever hereafter be rebuilt and that no division in consequence shall ever take place in the Parish;
> 2ndly, That the land upon which the chapel shall or may

be built shall be conveyed to the parish by deed, and not to any one or more persons or individuals of said parish;

3rdly, That whatever parish property the parish have or may hereafter have shall be appropriated for the benefit of the whole parish as it exists equally, and that neither the northern or the southern section of the parish shall have any particular or exclusive rights or privileges the one over the other, except that the Parish meetings shall be subject to be held at the old church if Required by at least five freeholders of the parish;

4thly, The Chapel shall be built by free donations and subscriptions of individuals who may feel disposed to contribute the same, and the parish, as a parish shall be in no way directly or indirectly subject to any tax or assessment for the expense of erecting said Chapel;

5thly, The whole parish jointly and severally shall hereafter be subject to any order they may feel disposed to take for the repairing of either the church or chapel as may hereafter be deemed expedient;

6thly, Whenever said Chapel shall be finished in decent style and convenient manner for the celebration of Worship of Almighty God according to the usage of the Protestant Episcopal Church it shall be entitled to one equal half of the services of the officiating or settled Clergyman not only on Sundays but on all feasts and fasts of the church and all other ordinary and extraordinary occasions;

7thly, No alteration or dispensation of any of the articles in this resolution shall ever hereafter be made so long as there remain ten respectable freeholders in the parish to object.

The terms were accepted. Captain Van Deusen donated much of the money needed to construct the chapel as well as the parcel of land on which it would be built: "bounded south on the Turnpike road and west on the east line of a country road laid out by the County Commissioners and not yet opened. The southwest corner of said Chapel is to be fifty feet distant in a northwardly direction from a black oak tree standing near the north line of said turnpike road."

On January 18, 1829, the vestry voted "that the chapel may have liberty to fix a bell in the chapel at Van Deusenville. Said bell to remain in said chapel for the use of the society so long as the present arrangements."

The bell that now hangs in the tower of the Guthrie Center was cast in 1835 in Holbrook, Massachusetts. Church records do not indicate whether it took six years to put a bell in the tower or this was the church's second bell, presumably reinstalled when the present edifice was constructed in 1866.

"With a view of accommodating the increasing population in the North part of the Society, they are now building a chapel at VanDeusenville," said an 1829 account. "This is of brick, 64 feet by 40. When this is completed it is expected that there will be preaching alternately in the church and in the chapel. The Baptists are to have the privilege of using this for a part of the time."

On Tuesday, July 21, 1829, at half past ten o'clock, the cornerstone was laid with masonic ceremonies. An iron box containing a history of the society, samples of currency, and other items that might be of interest to future historians was sealed inside the cornerstone. The order of service for the event was as follows:

> Divine Service will commence at the Hall at Van Deusenville at half past 10 o'clock A.M. The Masonic Procession will organize in the mean time at the house of Mr. Chace. After service the procession will form in the following order.
>
> 1. Gentlemen in general with the boys and young men in front.
>
> 2. Ladies Singers in the rear and the Gentlemen singers next in order.
>
> 3. Band of Music.
>
> 4. Masonic Procession in due form, with the Corner Stone, in the rear, under the conduct of the Master Workman and Master of the Lodge.
>
> 5. The Clergy.
>
> When the Procession arrives at the foundation, they will halt and open to the right and left, five paces distant. The Singers will then advance to the place appointed for them. The Procession will then counter march. Those who carry

the Corner Stone will advance and lay it upon the corner of the foundation.

ORDER OF THE SERVICE

1sr. Sing 68th Ps. 3d. Part, to verse 28th.

Min. O Lord the helper and protector of all who trust in thee, may thy blessing of grace and favor rest upon us.

Peo. As our eyes wait upon thee O Lord our God.

Min. Our help is in the name of the Lord.

Peo. Who hath made heaven and earth.

Min. Into thy merciful hands O God we commend the work of this building and all those who may be employed in the workmanship thereof.

Peo. May they be precious in thy sight, and may thy mercy be over the work of thy hands.

Min. In thy name O God — The Father, Son and Holy Ghost — lay the Corner Stone of thy Sanctuary to be erected on this foundation and consecrated to thy holy worship forever.

Peo. Amen. So may it be.

The Stone will then be plumb'd, squared and leveled. After which the service will conclude as follows —

Min. O Lord open thou our lips.

Peo. And our mouth shall show forth thy praise.

Min. Glory be to the Father, &c.

Peo. As it was in the beginning, is now, and ever shall be, world without end, Amen.

Min. O Lord hear our prayer.

Peo. And let our supplication come before thee.

A Prayer Follows. Sing five verses of 132nd Psalm. Then Follows the Address. Sing the 101st Hymn. The Blessing. Dine at Mr. Chaces.

The entire building was finished in less than a year, at a cost of $3448.76. It was consecrated October 27, 1830, by Alexander Viets Griswold, bishop of the Eastern Diocese, a nephew of the missionary Roger Viets. The bishop's ministry as head of a diocese that included all of New England except Connecticut was said to have greatly strengthened the Episcopal Church in the region.

With its own industry and its own church, Van Deusenville began to carve out its own identity. It was helped in no small part by the arrival of a pair of Connecticut industrialists. In 1833 Timothy Chittenden and John H. Coffing came to Van Deusenville and replaced the town's sawmill with a blast furnace for the manufacture of pig iron. The metal was used for guns, cannons, railroad tracks, and railroad-car wheels. Van Deusenville was the perfect location for such a furnace. The nearby quarries in West Stockbridge and Richmond provided a very high grade of ore. Once processed, the iron was hauled to the Hudson River, where it was loaded onto boats bound for New York City

Richmond Iron Works on Williams River in Van Deusenville.

The furnace later became part of the Richmond Iron Works, which improved the operation and made it a major source of employment for the village. In 1855 the business employed eight men to run the works and ten to twelve teams to draw the materials for the melting of the ore. It provided work for haulers, who brought charcoal from all parts of the county, and for woodsmen, who sold logs to the mill for burning. In very short order, most of the town was employed directly or indirectly by the iron works.

The works were run by John Henry Coffing, a second-generation iron man who was born in 1811. He was the third of nine children of Captain John C. Coffing of Holley & Coffing, a leading business in Salisbury. The younger John was sent to the best schools, including the Stockbridge Academy, whose principal at the time was Mark Hopkins, later president of Williams College. Yet he had, as the *Berkshire Courier* put it, "no desire for a college degree and a professional career." When he turned eighteen, John became a clerk in his father's company. As the company grew, he moved up in the ranks. In 1885 historian Charles J. Taylor described him:

> In matters of business, Mr. Coffing exercised sound judgement and great foresight, weighing carefully the subject presented, expressing his views with originality and clearness, and acting promptly and efficiently. Open and frank, proverbially truthful and honest himself, he would brook no duplicity or deceit in others. With more than ordinary mechanical skill, he combined good taste and an appreciation of the beautiful; he did well what he did, built well what he built, with always an eye to usefulness and durability. Benevolent and generous in his public contributions he was ever ready to assist in a worthy object. His private gifts to the needy were numerous, unostentatious, often unsolicited. Many young men have profited by his counsel, and many — whom he deemed worthy — have received substantial pecuniary aid. Mr. Coffing was sociable in conversation, with gravity for the grave, and humor for the humorous; he was quick to appreciate the ludicrous, and would often discover, under a rough garb, much that was admirable and to his liking. His attachments for his friends were strong; he entertained them bountifully; had nothing too good for them, and entered into their cares, wishes, and hopes as if they were his own.

In an obituary, the *Berkshire Courier* mentioned another side of his character: "Personally Mr. Coffing was genial, fond of conversation and a good story, and keen in his remarks. His honesty was a part of his very fibre, but as is so often the case with sternly upright men, he was sometimes wrong in his impressions of others, and occasionally cherished prejudices that were not always well founded." But, the writer added, "to all objects that his judgement approved Mr. Coffing was a generous giver. The beautiful chapel of Trinity Parish, Van Deusenville, was built largely by his aid."

John Coffing moved to Van Deusenville shortly after he married Rebecca Bostwick. He made his home in a large, pillared house built by Captain Van Deusen next to the church. So prominent was Coffing that the local newspaper often reported on his vacations. (After his death, the newspaper kept its readers abreast of his widow's vacations.) He had a great interest in politics and was once elected town assessor, a post he held for only two days. According to Taylor, "he found the duties and associates so uncongenial that he early and peremptorily abandoned it." He was a member of the Whig Party until it disbanded in the 1850s and was a delegate to the 1860 Republican national convention, which nominated Abraham Lincoln. During the War Between the States, John Coffing presided at town meetings held to recruit soldiers and raise money for the Union effort.

The growing importance of the railroad, and later the onset of the Civil War, made iron indispensable. The federal government wanted the best metal for its weapons, and it conducted a large-scale test of samples from a number of iron works to see which would make the best cannons. With his political connections, Coffing managed to have the Van Deusenville furnace's product included in the test. As a result, he secured a Union military contract. During the war, the government took almost all the output of the iron works. The operation accelerated to double shifts, pouring every twelve hours and employing more than a hundred men.

In her book *History of Richmond,* Katharine H. Annin suggested that the famous Union Navy ship the *Monitor* may have been made of the company's iron. "It seems likely," she wrote, "that Richmond [supplied] some iron for [its] plates. Also the two guns in her turret were in all probability made from Richmond iron."

The area became so busy that "the freight on the Housatonic Railroad necessitates the running of extra trains nearly every day. Monday there were 110 cars loaded waiting at Van Deusenville and West Stockbridge and yesterday some fifty or sixty more arrived," wrote the *Berkshire Courier.* "They are being forwarded to their destination as fast as possible. The extra heavy freight trains passed here yesterday. The travel of passengers is also very large at present."

The Van Deusenville railroad station was located on land leased by Trinity Church, partially visible at the far right.

Van Deusenville was booming, and the church was growing right along with it. With its newfound economic strength and the friendly rivalry with Great Barrington, it was not long before a "division of consequence" took place between the chapel and the parent church. For the first decade of its existence, the Van Deusenville church had shared the services of St. James's minister, the Reverend Sturges Gilbert. In the beginning, the minister would preach one week in Great Barrington, the next in Van Deusenville. Over time, however, the number of visits to Van Deusenville decreased. In spite of the provision that each church should have 50 percent of the services of the minister, the people of the St. James Parish decided that the preaching at the two churches should be in proportion to the amount of collections taken in at each. Consequently, the smaller church was given fewer services. The members of that church decided it was time to take charge of their own government.

On February 15, 1839, the parish met and voted that the Van Deusenville group could split from the parish provided that "the said Society of 'Trinity Church' and their successors shall use and occupy said Chapel for the purposes and object for which it was built and consecrated. But if ever said Society of Trinity Church, Van Deusenville, shall become extinct or shall fail to keep said Chapel in decent order for the maintenance of religious worship, agreeable to the form and usages of the Protestant Episcopal Church in the United States of America, then the said Chapel with the land and appurtenances thereto belonging shall revert to the original parent society."

The parishioners of Trinity chose their first wardens, Eber Stone and Isaac Van Deusen, and hired their first rector, Samuel P. Parker, the grandson and namesake of the second Episcopal bishop of Massachusetts. Along with preaching, Parker conducted a school for boys in Stockbridge for about twenty years. A parishioner wrote in 1805:

> Many of you can remember him as he stood in the church or walked the streets. His dignified presence, his snowy hair, his cultured voice, his light step are fresh in our recollection. He was a founder of churches, and as with many other founders and pioneers, much of his work is unknown to the world . . . His was a life of rigorous self-denial. He was a scholar, especially in the department of English literature which he loved to the very last. He was a builder-up of churches. A layer of foundations, he never despaired of the drudgery; he took infinite pains were his hearers few or many. He never relaxed, even in old age, his vigilant conscientiousness as a parish priest.

After years of division, first from the Congregationalists, then from the St. James Parish, Parker introduced a spirit of cooperation to the church. In his view, the goal of the Episcopal Church was "to reconcile all Christians in one all-embracing fellowship."

"On the separation of Trinity Church, Van Deusenville, in 1839, from the mother parish, Bishop Griswold sent me to take charge of the new parish," Parker would later recall. "There had been an interregnum in the services, and during this interregnum, the chapel at Van Deusenville had been granted to our friends, the Methodists. On the first Sunday of my rectorship, on arriving at the church door, a young Methodist clergyman occupied the desk by mistake. Our people asked me what they should do. 'Follow me,' I replied, 'and unite with our friends in their worship.' They all took my advice."

Shortly thereafter, the women of the church formed the Ladies' Benevolent Society of the Trinity Church. The society had sixty members, forty-nine women and eleven men, including many Van Deusens and most of the area's prominent women. They paid membership dues of 12 $^1/_2$ cents per year. The society held a number of well-attended social events, including festivals, "orange teas," and "strawberry dinners," to raise money for their charitable works. A Ladies' Sewing Circle was also formed that year. The women made clothes for a missionary to take to the poor and raised money to support the church.

In his annual report to the diocese, Samuel Parker wrote: "The church is the only house of worship in the village and neighborhood, and is active, and has opportunity for doing much good. May God finish the work he has begun."

In 1842 another society, the Washington Temperance Society of Van Deusenville, was formed. Most of its 290 teetotaling members were highly active in Trinity Church. The society secretary apparently kept minutes not only of the meetings but of the behavior of society members in the community. Members who were caught in the possession of "spiritous liquors" were expelled. Occasionally they would be allowed to return after promising to reform their wicked ways.

When Parker left Trinity in 1843, he told the diocese that the minister who followed him would find "an affectionate people to appreciate his labors."

By the mid-1840s, Trinity Church in Van Deusenville was sufficiently well established to come to the rescue of Trinity Church in Lenox, Massachusetts. The latter Trinity was "close to extinction," with no rector and a dwindling membership. In 1846 the Reverend S. T. Carpenter of Van Deusenville officiated in Lenox one Sunday a month. In 1848 the Reverend F. A. Foxcroft offered his services.

Meanwhile, with a seemingly endless need for iron, Van Deusenville was becoming important enough to vie with Great Barrington for the first bank in the area and a town hall. In addition to the iron works, there were now a chair manufacturing operation, a wagon shop, a sawmill, a gristmill, a rope walk, and a third store. In 1852 the church built a residence for the rector. Although Great Barrington won the battle to have the first bank and town hall, there was no reason to believe Van Deusenville and Trinity Church would do anything but grow.

FROM THE COLLECTION OF ROBERTA PERRY, COURTESY OF GARY LEVEILLE

From left: Irene Bostwick, Fanny Bostwick's mother; Mrs. Dobbs; Sarah Burgett. Van Deusenville, 1890s. Irene Bostwick was organist for a time at the Sunday 3 p.m. service at Trinity Church.

"Trinity Church, Van Deusenville, may pride itself on an interior which for gracefulness, and ease for the voice, is hardly equaled by any edifice in the state west of the Connecticut river."

— Reverend Samuel P. Parker

Van Deusenville, 1866

On April 2, 1866, President Andrew Johnson proclaimed "the insurrection which heretofore existed in the states of Georgia, South Carolina, Virginia, North Carolina, Tennessee, Alabama, Louisiana, Arkansas, Mississippi and Florida is at an end."

For the nation, it was a time of reconstruction and the beginning of the postwar prosperity that Mark Twain would label "The Gilded Age." Immigrants were coming to the country in record numbers. Between 1840 and 1890 the U.S. population quadrupled. In Massachusetts a mood of great optimism prevailed, as witnessed by this editorial in the *Berkshire Courier*:

> A Fast Age — It is truly astonishing to think what a fast age we are now living in. What numbers of wonderful enterprises have been conceived of, tested and fully developed, within the recollection of men still in the active business life.

Witness the hundred of ingenious and predictable ways of turning the power of steam to man's advantage; besides the steamboats and railroads; the wonderful achievement of the telegraph across the ocean and around the world; the great velocity at which knowledge is now spread abroad with printing-presses capable of throwing off 25,000 sheets an hour, instead of three hundred, as was the case a few years since; the extensive use of coal for fuel, instead of wood; the illuminating gas, and kerosene lights instead of the tallow dips. And still the cry is —"Onward."

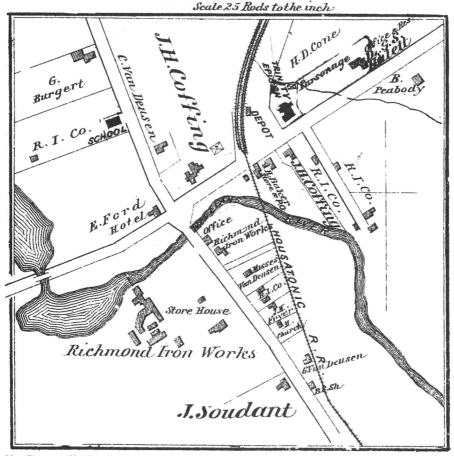

Van Deusenville circa 1876.

The late 1800s were also a period of growth for the Episcopal Church in the Commonwealth of Massachusetts. "Many in Massachusetts were no longer attracted to Calvinism or conservative Protestantism," writes John Allen Gable in his history of Trinity Church in Lenox. "But (they) found liberal Unitarianism, which had its stronghold in Massachusetts, to be at odds with Biblical Christianity. Significant numbers of the descendants of the Pilgrims and Puritans found a home in the Episcopal Church."

For Trinity Church, too, 1866 was a time of reconstruction. With a growing community to serve, the stone chapel had become too small years before. As early as 1861, then-minister Lewis Green reported to the diocese: "The church is greatly in need of repairs, or of being rebuilt. Some measures towards rebuilding were commenced last Fall, but owing to the disturbed state of affairs throughout the country, they have been remitted for the present." A year later the new rector, J.A. Penniman, wrote, "This parish requires a new house of worship, the necessity is imperative."

But the war had prevented any building for the next couple of years. Now that it was over, and with generous donations from prominent citizens like next-door neighbor John Coffing, a new church could be built to seat two hundred. The parish voted to "build a new church forthwith . . . after the plan of the Stockbridge Church with discriminatory powers to make such alterations as may be thought desirable for the accommodation of the Parish."

In August 1866, the stone church was torn down to make way for the construction of the new. When the builders lifted the original cornerstone, they were met with a surprise. As the *Courier* reported: "The box containing the records, papers &c. has not been found beneath the corner stone, and it is believed that it must have been stolen years ago — perhaps by the workmen who built the church."

The new building, built by J. A. McArthur and mason Isaac Barthram, was modeled after St. Paul's Church in Stockbridge, of which Samuel Parker was also the first rector. (This was the old version of St. Paul's, built in 1840. The current structure was built in 1884.) That church, also a pine structure, had been the design of Richard Upjohn. An important architect of the Gothic Revival movement, Upjohn was born in England and came to the United States in 1829. He is best known for his 1839 design of Trinity Church on Wall Street in New York City. After that success, he turned his attention to rural country churches, designing buildings that would be inexpensive but "correct in ecclesiological terms." The Episcopal Church, with its roots in England, mandated Gothic-style buildings in which each element contained religious symbolism--modern versions of the impressive medieval cathedrals that were artists' visions of what heaven might look like.

Designs for the new Trinity Church were based on this building, St. Paul's Church in Stockbridge, as it appeared in the 1840s.

COURTESY OF THE STOCKBRIDGE LIBRARY, STOCKBRIDGE, MASSACHUSETTS

In 1852 the architect published a book called *Upjohn's Rural Architecture*, which was used by many rural churches. A University of Massachusetts student, Christy Jo Anderson, wrote about the architect in 1982 in her history of St. Paul's Church. "Upjohn's small wooden churches reflect the American translation of the English parish church. The Rural Church, with its vertical siding, battering, and steep roofs, fulfilled the need for 'a rural church which is a model of economy, beauty, and convenience.'"

Trinity's new home was a pine structure with chestnut pews and fixtures. John Coffing personally supervised the construction and pitched in the majority of the $14,000 price tag. The west wall of the church was engraved with the dates and the names of pastors and builders of the two churches. The cornerstone of the old building, less the papers that had mysteriously disappeared, was used in the wooden structure's foundation. This was fitting for a building whose very architecture is a symbol of destruction and renewal.

The arched doorway and the general triangular shape of the building represent the three sides of the Trinity. The triangle can also be seen as pointing to heaven. Seen from above, less the bell tower, two spaces off the side of the sanctuary jut out and create a cross shape. The shape was no accident. When a worshiper entered the sanctuary, he or she walked through the central part of the church, or nave, and approached the altar. The word "nave" is derived from the Latin *navis*, which means "ship," thought to symbolize Noah's ark. The ark, which saved creation that it might be reborn after the flood, stands for, in the words of Saint Ambrose, the "power to preserve all things and ensure their rebirth."

Leading up to the front door and to the altar were three steps, which also represented the Trinity. Behind the altar, a high vaulted arch represented heaven. Thus, worshipers taking Communion walked through the nave with the arms of the cross surrounding them. The metaphorical path to heaven was through Christ's sacrifice, his death and rebirth.

The three sides of the arched stained-glass windows also symbolized the Trinity. The windows near the altar featured chalices, crosses, and lilies. With its three petals, the lily is also reminiscent of the Trinity and of the triple virtues of faith, hope, and charity. According to Christian tradition, the lily sprang from the tears of repentance Eve shed as she and Adam left the Garden of Eden after sampling the fruit of the tree of the knowledge of good and evil. The rose window in the front of the building depicts Matthew, Mark, Luke, and John.

The bell tower had a rectangular steeple into which the bell, cast in 1835 in Holbrook, Massachusetts, was placed. A ten-stall stable was built behind the church for parishioners' horses.

There is no official record of why the congregation decided to replace stone with wood, but Pierce Middleton speculates that strong postwar employment may have been the deciding factor. Before the Civil War the nation had suffered an economic depression. Because work was scarce, it was possible to hire masons for relatively little money. After the war there was work again, but also inflation. The impressive stone edifice of St. James Church that now stands in Great Barrington was built before the war and cost only a thousand dollars more to construct than

47

Trinity's wooden building.

The new church was consecrated by Bishop Manton Eastburn on September 24, 1868. Of the new building Samuel Parker said, "Trinity Church, Van Deusenville, may pride itself on an interior which for gracefulness, and ease for the voice, is hardly equaled by any edifice in the state west of the Connecticut river."

Years later F. C. Lindley, whose great-grandfather had been a warden and who himself was a treasurer of the church around the time of World War I, said it was "as rich a church as you can find."

Yet, while there were a few wealthy and prominent supporters to outfit the church with the best of everything, the majority of the church-goers were working men and women. They were the people who shoveled coal into the furnaces, raised families, ran the stores, and hauled iron and wood to and from the mills.

The annual report to the diocese for 1874 described the state of the church and spoke of Reverend Parker, who had returned to the congregation:

> The interior of the Trinity Church, Van Deusenville, is the most beautiful in Southern Berkshire. The parish owns a respectable parsonage and glebe [land]. The Rector ministered to their fathers and mothers in this Parish, some 30 years since, and now he has entered into a pastoral relation with their children. There are many old members religiously attached to our church. The edifice at Van Deusenville is the only house of worship within two or three miles, and the church is doing good work, gathering the poor and neglected. The services are growing in fervor. The attendance is improving. Outsiders are coming in. Congregational singing is increasing the religious interest. A sewing society is working spiritedly for the church and for the Indians.

Every Sunday the bell would ring, announcing the nine-thirty service. Another service was held in the afternoon. They were sometimes sparsely attended during the harsh New England winters, but in the summer services were often packed. Sometimes, in the early days, services were so crowded that extra chairs had to be put in the aisles. The farmers and the well-to-do would arrive in horse and carriage and leave the horses in the stable. Most churchgoers simply walked.

They arrived in their Sunday best. For the ladies this meant fashionable attire, but not too fashionable. A new, slightly shocking style called "bloomers" was all the rage, and there was some discussion as to whether short skirts were appropriate attire for the church. One Lexington, Massachusetts, educator wrote an editorial in praise of the attire: "Indeed, some of the clergymen, who observed that our young ladies changed for the long dress on going to church, came to me to say that they hoped I would allow them to come in their short dresses, for they liked very much to see them."

The ladies of the Ladies Aid Society, of course, would not have been seen in bloomers. They were expected to be perfectly proper at all times. If they were caught drinking hard cider, they were asked to leave the group.

"The fair and festival of the ladies of Trinity Church, Van Deusenville, on Wednesday evening of last week, was largely attended, and was one of the pleasantest social gatherings of the winter," the *Courier* reported in March 1880. "Goodly delegations were present from this village and the neighborhood round about was well represented. The net earnings of the evening were $82, of which sum $29 was raised by the children's table."

That year, the Easter offering took in $33.64, which the newspaper reported was "a gratifying evidence of the prosperity of Trinity Parish."

It was not all temperance, teas, and sewing circles. The community also celebrated heartily when the occasion arose. In 1915 the *Pittsfield Journal* looked back on the 1865 wedding of Fred Burghardt and Emma Frances Eden on the occasion of their fiftieth anniversary. The wedding had taken place in the bride's home and was officiated by the Reverend J. A. Penniman of Trinity.

> The ceremony was performed at 8 o'clock P.M. and the house was thronged with friends of the young people for the bride was but 17, and many congratulations were showered upon the happy couple. They made more of marriage at that time than they seem to do today. From the surrounding countryside the young people gathered and the send-off that was given the bridal couple has lingered among the pleasant memories of half a century. Nor did it end with that occasion. The night following at the home of the bridegroom's parents

in the Long Pond district, came a repetition of the festivities. Again did the countryside pour into the hospitable home of the Burghardts its throng of merrymakers, and the very rafters rang with the mirth and merriment which followed. Until the wee small hours of morning the festivities continued and it was thus this happy couple were launched upon their matrimonial voyage.

In 1880 the Western Convocation of the Episcopal Church was held in Great Barrington. The two-day program was concluded at Trinity. The Reverend Lewis Green of Ashfield, who was rector of the parish from 1848 to 1861 and the only priest to be ordained at Trinity Van Deusenville, preached for the first time in the present church edifice. His sermon was said to have spoken affectionately of those with whom he formerly ministered, and it was a touching moment for the congregation. He would preach at the building only one more time. He returned in 1882 to perform the funeral service for John Coffing.

The Young Ladies Trinity Guild became active around this time. They collected money to purchase a "beautiful and substantial" lectern for the church. The church also added a portable pipe organ, which, the report to the diocese said, "added very much to the interest of the music."

Trinity even spawned its own short-lived mission, the Housatonic Mission, established on Christmas Day, 1893. It was formed to serve the portion of the population that was slowly migrating north. For about a year, services were held in the Central Block, Housatonic, for about sixty members. When it closed, roughly a third of its members returned to Trinity Church. In 1895 Trinity's membership rose to 192 active communicants.

Two years later, the iron furnace closed.

"My heart will always be with Trinity. It was God's church, and we loved it."

— Mary Sachs, last clerk of
Trinity Church

Great Barrington, 1999

"There's not a window in my house that doesn't look out on the church," says Mary Sachs.

The last clerk of Trinity Church, now eighty-nine, still lives in the house in which she was born. She can even show you the very spot, in the middle of the kitchen, where that event occurred. A large framed drawing of the church hangs on the wall of her living room, which looks out on the real church. In the window are two flower-shaped pieces of stained glass, mementos that were once part of the windows of her beloved church.

Mary hates it when people call it "Alice's Church" or "Arlo's Church." When the newspaper refers to the landmark that way, she writes a letter to the editor. "Alice wasn't a minister. She never preached there. After all, it was the church where I worshiped. If it had been a church where you worshiped and Arlo came along, you wouldn't like it either."

51

COLLECTION OF MARY SACHS

The brown-painted Trinity Church circa 1940. It was this color when Mary Sachs attended services.

Mary was confirmed at Trinity. Her son was baptized there. Her sister taught Sunday School. She remembers the black walnut trees that once lined the church property. She remembers where she sat for services, two or three seats from the back on the right. She remembers the children reading poems, exchanging presents by the tree at Christmas. She is filled with nostalgia for the children's choir when she hears the old familiar songs. "When they sing the songs at St. James, I love them: 'Onward Christian Soldiers,' 'Stand Up, Stand Up for Jesus.'"

When Mary attended church, it was open only during the warm

months, which in Massachusetts meant it was closed most of the year. "If there were six people at the church it was a good day," she remembers. It was a far cry from the days when extra chairs had to be brought in to seat all the parishioners.

Mary remembers the rickety stairs that led up to the bell tower and helping her father ring the bell. Mary's parents, Louis and Louise Stickles, were not rich and prominent like the Coffings or Van Deusens. They could not afford to give a lot of money to their church, but they wanted to contribute however they could. So Louis volunteered to be the church caretaker. He was in charge of the furnace and ringing that massive bell. Several years later, Mary took over for her father and became the last person to care for Trinity Church and its property.

Van Deusenville, a one-industry town, did not survive the loss of the iron works. As Mary Sachs put it, "I know I live in Van Deusenville, but most people don't anymore."

It has been widely reported by some very reputable sources, including George Edwin MacLean's extension to 1922 of *The History of Great Barrington*, that Van Deusenville's furnace exploded in 1897 and was never reopened. It is a colorful image and a fitting, dramatic conclusion to the life of the village. But neither Trinity Church records nor the *Berkshire Courier* of 1897 make any reference to an accident at the furnace. A 1922 article in the *Courier* written on the occasion of the removal of the last furnace buildings (ironically by the contractor who had put the last lining in the furnace in 1889) simply reports that "about 25 years ago it was decided to close up the industry."

The furnace probably did not go up in a ball of flame. Instead, the economic forces that had fanned the flames of the iron works shifted, and those flames quickly went out.

It took a lot of charcoal and a lot of manpower to run the various branches of the Richmond Iron Works — about 120 to 125 bushels of charcoal to make a ton of iron. As the nineteenth century drew to a close, the price of charcoal soared. Organized labor gained strength, and wages began to rise. Workers at the Richmond Iron Works received $1 to $1.50 for a ten- to twelve-hour day. Toward the turn of the century, wages rose to as much as $4 a day. As iron became more expensive to produce, the Bessemer process for making steel was also reducing the price of iron.

Around this time, a great iron range was discovered in Minnesota.

Other mines in Lake Superior, Wisconsin, produced 60 to 65 percent metallic iron, compared to 42 percent in Massachusetts. Not only was midwestern ore purer than the Berkshire variety, it was also easier and cheaper to transport to the new industrial centers in the Midwest, where it was used in an up-and-coming industry — the manufacture of automobiles.

Meanwhile, thriving businesses in the neighboring village of Housatonic were drawing people in that direction. In 1871 the Reverend Frederic A. Fiske wrote, "As the village of Housatonic, two miles distant, is increasing and rapidly extending its business towards us, already having approached within a mile, where a very large paper mill and numerous dwellings are soon to be erected, the hope of the growth of Trinity Parish seems to lie in that direction." In fact, Housatonic came to them. The former Van Deusenville church is now considered to be in Housatonic. Division Street, once known as the Albany Turnpike, is so named because it divides Housatonic from Great Barrington. Where Mary Sachs lives, across the street from the church, is Great Barrington proper.

By 1890 the iron works were experiencing long work stoppages. The minister wrote: "Owing to the stoppage of the Furnace here for a long time, several families whose children attended the Sunday School have moved away. The one thousand dollars used 'For Improvement of Property' might in this case be more correctly expressed 'For Preservation and Improvement of Property.'"

By 1896 there was already discussion as to whether the church should continue its afternoon service. That year the parishioners voted to keep the second service, but it would not continue for long. If there was one year that marked the end for Van Deusenville and the beginning of the end for Trinity Church, it was 1897. That year Eveline Stone Burgert's sister passed away. Eveline traveled by train to Syracuse to collect her sister's remains so a funeral could be held at the church built in part by their father, Eber Stone. On March 19, "the last of the Isaac Van Deusens" died. He was followed a week later by his wife. The *Berkshire Courier* announced the losses:

> Our village has been called to mourn over the departure of two of our estimable elderly people who have long been residents of the hamlet within a short time, their deaths occurring within a week. In the last issue The Courier chronicled the death

of the husband, little thinking the wife was so soon to follow. On Tuesday of last week the funeral of Isaac Van Deusen was attended in Trinity Church, Rev. F. A. Foxcroft officiating. The following day, 11 o'clock p.m. the spirit of his wife departed and she, too, was at rest. Pneumonia did its fatal work and their home was made desolate by the fell destroyer. Mrs. Van Deusen was the youngest daughter of the late Milton and Abigail Ball of Stockbridge. Three of the Ball family married into the family of Deacon Isaac Van Deusen. Mrs. Van Deusen's funeral was largely attended at Trinity Church Sunday afternoon and the interment was in the lower cemetery in Housatonic, by the side of her husband. Mrs. Van Deusen was a very hospitable woman, an excellent hostess, always giving her visitors a hearty welcome. She was a communicant of the Episcopal church and was always present unless detained by ill health. Mrs. Van Patten, their only child, has the sincere sympathy of her many friends in her double bereavement.

If you would like to pay your respects to some of the people whose lives are so closely associated with Trinity Church, you can still visit the graves of the original Isaac Van Deusen and his kin at the Van Deusen Cemetery. It is located on what was once Isaac's property in Great Barrington on Route 183 just south of Division Street. The cemetery was begun when the first Isaac Van Deusen lost his youngest daughter, Gesie. He buried her in the yard of his manor house. Later his wife was buried there, and it remained the family's private burial ground until 1819, when it was moved to the town. Not everyone was pleased with that decision. Louis Hasbrouck Sahler, author of *The History and Genealogy of the Van Deusens of Van Deusen Manor,* wrote: "The family should not have allowed their ancestral burial ground to pass out of the family and become the sepulcher of promiscuous people."

After stopping at the markers for Isaac the Rich and kin, you may wish to look toward the south and take a moment to remember the people who passed through life without leaving any monuments behind. The early Dutch settlers of Massachusetts were slave owners. The slaves were buried near their masters on the south side of the grounds, outside the fence, in unmarked graves.

A month after the last Isaac Van Deusen died, the iron works were closed for good. "Teams are hauling coal and ore from the furnace, which looks as if Van Deusenville is doomed to rest in quietude for some time to come," the newspaper reported.

A month after that, the paper had another loss to report: "Rev. F. A. Foxcroft has notified the officers of Trinity Church of his resignation, which will close his connection with them about Sept. 1. Mr. Foxcroft came to this parish about four years ago, and several of our citizens connected with the welfare of the church and society have since died, leaving only a comparatively few to give it support. We understand that he has accepted a call in Beechwood."

In 1900 a special meeting was called "for the election of officers and to consider whether this parish should remain as heretofore." It was decided that the parish would not remain as heretofore. Instead it would, while maintaining its independence, share the services of the minister of St. James.

Given this turn of events, it is surprising that Trinity Church survived into the 1960s, but there was something about the place that engendered a stubborn loyalty in many of its parishioners — people like Mary Sachs; the Louis Faivre family, who may have had little money but gave of their time and hearts; and the wealthy relatives of John Coffing, who perhaps saw the church as the last symbol of Coffing's thriving industrial village.

Back in the days when Mary was cleaning the church, she wanted to be sure to do a good job for Fanny Coffing Bostwick. Fanny wasn't officially her boss, but in many ways the church was hers. She was the financial force keeping the church alive in the first part of the twentieth century. Mary Sachs remembers Fanny Bostwick as "a prim and proper old maid." She was involved in a number of community organizations, including the Salisbury Association in Salisbury, Connecticut, whence the Coffings hailed. The association had a mission very similar to Arlo Guthrie's later vision for his nonprofit organization, the Guthrie Center. According to a book prepared by the Salisbury Association in 1913, "The Association stands for cooperation in all civic matters that may properly be fostered by it, without duplicating or interfering with the activities of other existing organizations that are necessarily more limited in their scope."

When John Coffing passed away in 1882, his wife had had a plaque mounted in the church, where it remains to this day. "In loving memory of John H. Coffing," it reads, "this tablet is erected by his wife, Rebecca F. Coffing." She also had a mortuary chapel built in his honor at the Pittsfield Hospital. The $1,400 chapel included an autopsy room, an audience room, chairs, and a reading desk.

The buildings and plaques would be the only things to carry on the Coffings' name. They had no children and therefore no direct heirs. When Rebecca died, their niece, Fanny Bostwick, inherited much of the family fortune, including the impressive Coffing house. The daughter of Rebecca's brother, Henry Bostwick, Fanny was born in 1865. In her formative years she lived in a thriving Van Deusenville with a new church building at the center of the community. She would have attended the christenings, weddings, and funerals of family and friends at the church. She was thirty-two years old when her uncle's iron furnace closed and Van Deusenville's population began to shrink. In her will Rebecca Coffing had left a trust fund for the church, which Fanny administered. Fanny also aided the church with her own substantial assets. She never married, and with no children of her own it is possible that she saw the church as her only family legacy.

In 1903 someone suggested closing the church for the winter and holding meetings in the sewing room because of the expense of heating the sanctuary. Fanny Bostwick was one of the parishioners who opposed that measure. "Decision not made," the church logs record. A donation of $50 by the B. D. Rising Paper Company briefly postponed the inevitable, and for a short time there was renewed enthusiasm in the church. The vestry voted to buy six tons of coal, and vestryman W. H. Hubbart was asked to "secure the same amount of the Great Barrington Coal Company." Vestryman Irving L. White was chosen to find "a man to build fires and ring the bell for four months commencing in December." The next year the vestry bought $8 1/2$ tons of coal to heat the church and decided to look into painting the rectory. "Miss Fannie Bostwick appointed a committee of one," the record said.

By December 1907, however, the cold finally defeated the church members. They decided to close the church in January, February, and March. During those months, Sunday School was held in private homes.

In 1910 Fanny's sister, Louise Bostwick, passed away. Her passing was significant enough to be recorded in the church logs.

Forasmuch as it has pleased almighty God in his infinite wisdom to take unto himself the soul of Miss M. Louise Bostwick and whereas by her death this church has lost a faithful worker and an earnest supporter and whereas in her sad death this church has lost an efficient and faithful treasurer who served in that capacity for many years, whereas the members of this church have lost a staunch friend, therefore be it resolved — that we, the rector, wardens, vestry and people of Trinity Parish, which submitting to the will of our Heavenly Father deeply mourn the loss of our beloved sister and extend to her bereaved mother and sister our deepest sympathy.

That same year marked the end of another era for the church. After 1910, Trinity would no longer have a priest of its own. Until 1960, when services were no longer held at the church, the St. James rectors would also be "vicars of Trinity."

The last priest of Trinity Van Deusenville was Howard Murray Dumbell II. He was born in England and educated by a governess and tutors. The family emigrated to the United States in 1876 and settled in Texas, where the elder Dumbell bought a large ranch near the Mexican border. Two years later Howard Sr. became an Episcopal priest and built a number of churches in Tennessee. Howard Jr. not only carried his father's name but also followed in his footsteps. He attended the Theological Seminary at the University of the South in Sewanee, Tennessee, and was ordained in 1891. He became a U.S. citizen shortly after moving to Great Barrington in 1899. "He came to his service as a clergyman with deep-rooted principles as well as an admirable mental equipment," wrote Hamilton Child in the *Berkshire County Gazetteer*. "He has endeared himself to his people perhaps more closely than had he been 'native here and to the manner born,' though it is to be said he is a thorough American by free choice and out of an ardent appreciation of American institutions and opportunities for usefulness."

Now, without a priest of its own, the church had come full circle. It was once again "a chapel in continuation with the parent church."

The cost of heating the cavernous building continued to be a problem for the dwindling church membership. In 1912 the massive coal

Trinity Church with its steeple, circa 1950.

PHOTO BY GLADYS WATSON, COURTESY OF THE DIOCESE OF WESTERN MASSACHUSETTS

furnaces in the basement broke down, so along with the $72.25 spent on coal and the $25.50 for a man to stoke the fire, the church had to spend another $186.16 to repair the furnaces.

Sometime around 1920, the church's gas lighting was replaced with electricity, courtesy of the Rebecca Coffing Trust. In 1931 Fanny Bostwick donated money to install new coal furnaces in the church basement, and in 1937 the church record states: "It was voted that Miss Bostwick be continued as a special furnace committee."

But it was still cold in the church. The exact dates of operation changed from year to year, based presumably on the weather. The church sometimes closed for the season as early as October and opened as late as July.

The parish journal said that "so small was the attendance and so few the services being held, that no annual meeting was called for the years 1929 and 1930." The next year Fanny insisted on a meeting, and from then until shortly before her death the meetings were held in her home. Each gathering was capped with a social hour and refreshments.

Even the "Rebecca fund," as it came to be called, and Fanny Bostwick's donations were not enough to keep the church property from shrinking. In 1940 the church sold the land it had leased to the railroad, which now housed only an abandoned station. The selling price was $50 and a letter "assuring us the land will be kept in an orderly condition."

Beginning in 1942, the annual meetings were moved from Fanny Bostwick's home to the home of Mrs. Louis Faivre. Four years later Fanny passed away, leaving an estate of about $500,000. She left $10,000, in memory of her mother, Irene J. Bostwick, and her sister, Louise Bostwick, to the Episcopal Diocese of Western Massachusetts to be used to maintain Trinity Church. Because she died in January, when Trinity was closed, Fanny Bostwick's funeral was held at St. James.

After her death, Trinity had one more regular summer season. That year the church was painted; this is probably when it went from brown to white. In 1947 (the year Arlo Guthrie was born) regular services ceased. The church served about ten families with three or four services a year and occasional special events; there was at least one wedding there as late as 1956.

Even in these times, however, the Van Deusenville church had an impact on the community. "You should see the bell. It's huge," Mary says. "When Bobby Faivre came out of the service [at the end of World War II] we all took turns ringing it. He was a handsome young boy. He meant a lot to everyone. We all loved him. When he came out of the service we rang the bell for about three days. We rang it morning, noon, and night."

Neighbor Diana Harwood, who now runs a bed and breakfast in John Coffing's old estate next to the church, vividly remembers the bell. "When I was a girl, they'd show clips from the war in newsreels. I didn't understand that was going on so far away and not across the street. You can't understand that when you're young. It was terrifying. When the war ended, I was sitting out on the lawn and bells started ringing. I asked my brother what they were for. He said, 'You stupid fool, the war ended.' When I heard the bells ringing I knew everything would be all right."

She also remembers one of the neighbors, Bessie Beckwith, who would dress up for church whenever there was a service. Her husband, who did not attend, would drive her to church in a horse and carriage. "Mr. Beckwith would hook up his horse and carriage, and she'd have a big flowered hat on," Diana says. "I always wanted to go, but we were Catholic. I couldn't understand the difference then. A church was a church. I'd just sit there on the lawn and say [to my parents], 'Please let me go to church with them.'"

As the church fell into disuse, the rotting steeple became a home for owls, which neighbors say you

This Christmas card, printed around 1954, shows the deterioration of the steeple. The embellishments at the top of the tower have all fallen down or been removed.

COLLECTION OF MARY SACHS

could hear all night long. The remaining parishioners tried putting chicken wire around the steeple's openings to keep the birds out, but to no avail. It was dilapidated and dangerous and had to come down. Because they could not afford to rebuild the structure, it was replaced with the hip roof — a wooden pyramid with small aluminum side louvers — that now covers the bell tower.

There is an entertaining story about the removal of the steeple. As the story goes, various contractors put in bids on the job of removing the top of the tower. Several estimated it would cost hundreds of dollars to take it down with a crane. Then Alfred "Bud" Van Deusen came along and said, "Hell, I can take it down for seventy-five dollars." He went up to the steeple with a chain saw and in a few minutes sawed around the base of the structure and pulled it down with a rope.

Historian Bernard Drew asked Bud's widow, Eleanor, about the anecdote when he was researching his updated version of the *History of Great Barrington*. She didn't remember the specific episode, but she told him that her husband did do work on church steeples. Those who knew Bud Van Deusen say it would have been in character for him. The church issued several checks to Alfred Van Deusen around this time, but what they were for, the story of how he was chosen, and how the task was completed are not recorded. In any case, the checks amounted to more than $75 and probably paid for both removing the steeple and building the current roof.

"The church still needs more work," vestryman Louis E. Faivre told a *Berkshire Eagle* reporter in 1955, "but as long as I'm around, I'm going to do all I can to keep it going."

In 1958 Mary Sachs submitted a working budget of "$0" to the diocese. "The Church operates 4 Sundays per year and expenses are paid from invested funds," she wrote.

Over the next five years Louis Faivre's dedication to keep the church going waned. It was a matter of simple economics. It cost more to keep the church in repair than the ten loyal families could collect. It was rarely open and rarely maintained. In 1962 the last meeting of the church officers — senior warden Louis Faivre, treasurer Paul White, and clerk Mary Sachs — was held at Mary's home.

"They were getting old," Mary says. "There were no new people coming to live here. People had automobiles, so they could go to Great Barrington. There was not enough money coming in. I was there because I was an officer. They made the decision [to sell the church]. I didn't say anything."

Mary asked the church warden if she could have the small church organ, a pedal organ with a little shelf to hold candles. (Apparently there were two church organs, because they honored her request but an organ was also sold with the building.)

"I loved the organ," she says. "I loved the church. One day I stopped down in Robert K. Wheeler's office. I said, 'I'm very poor and I'd love to have the organ.' He said he'd talk it over with the others. I tried to learn how to play it, but I couldn't." The organ is now in Connecticut in the home of Mary's grandson. She says her eleven-year-old great-grandson, Kevin, is an impressive musician. He plays the organ, piano, and trumpet.

Mary's fondness for the old church is clear every time she speaks. Today she attends St. James Church. She says the services there are just like the ones at Trinity. "St. James is beautiful. But my feelings will always be for Trinity. It was God's church, and we loved it."

She did not attend the deconsecration ceremony. Weeks later she was shocked to see long-haired youths in strange clothes driving their motorcycles up a ramp and right through the church door.

The sanctuary around 1963, shortly after Ray and Alice Brock moved in.

PAUL KLEINWALD

"So I went up and I saw Ray. There was only one thing Ray could say . . ."

— Arlo Guthrie
"The Motorcycle Song"

Housatonic, 1963

T he church was a sanctuary, and you knew it right away," says Rick Robbins, who first visited Ray and Alice Brock's church in 1963, when he was seventeen. "The first time I went there I was on my motorcycle. I said to Ray, 'Do you have something I can use to cover up this motorcycle?' He said, 'No, bring it inside!' So we got a ramp and brought the motorcycle inside, and right then I knew--this place is great. Here's my motorcycle in the sanctuary of this great building. We never once thought about it being sacrilegious to do all that. It just didn't have that vibe. It was just perfect. This is a perfect place to get away from everything."

As the iron furnace was to Trinity Church, Alice and Ray Brock were to the people who would congregate in the building in the 1960s. The Brocks were the flame that drew a community and gave it its reason for being. On the surface the new community would be about as different from the old as it was possible to be. There would be no structure, no High Mass, no rules of living, and very little ceremony. This is not to say that it was devoid of a philosophy. The group would share a set of common, if unwritten, views on life, views that were a product of the times and of their youth, social background, education, and the shared values that all groups of friends create.

The church was to be the kind of place where everyone was welcome. You could stay as long as you needed to. Alice would cook you a meal that was probably better than anything Mom used to make. It was a place where you could let your hair down — no matter how long it was. Most of all it was a place for friends to gather and play music and enjoy each other's company.

The door was always open, because Ray and Alice were open-door kind of people. If someone had written the philosophy of their new sanctuary it might have sounded similar to Reverend Parker's statement that "the most excellent way of spreading the truth, first, midst, last, is charity towards those who are different from us."

"They seemed to have an enthusiasm for living life," says Paul Kleinwald, a Stockbridge School classmate of Arlo's. "They were very generous and welcoming. If I called and just showed up and needed a place to stay, I'd have one, whether they had a bed or I wanted to roll up on the floor in a pile of blankets."

One writer described the group as being "like early Christians." As Alice puts it, "They had a ceremony to take God out of the church before we moved in, as though you can pick God up and place him here or there. I don't feel like the church was deconsecrated. It was always a holy place."

Ray Brock, twelve years Alice's senior, was a divorced father of three when the pair met. He was tall, six foot two, with dark curly hair and eyes that conveyed a special intensity. A native of Hampton, Virginia, Ray spoke with a slight southern accent. He enjoyed old country, folk, and bluegrass music. One of his favorite songs was "T. is for Texas" by Jimmie Rodgers. Woody Guthrie was another favorite artist. Thanks to the GI Bill, Ray was the first in his family to earn an advanced degree. He studied architecture at the University of Virginia and did corporate architectural work for a number of years, but he had a fiery temperament that did not adapt easily to life in a suit and tie.

"Ray was a trained architect — that was his real job — but he was also an incredible carpenter," Arlo says. "I don't mean 'carpenter' in the normal sense, but he was a sculptor. He had huge pieces of wood that he would chisel into these incredible shapes. So he was a real artist, but at the same time there are buildings here in town that he designed for a living, the typical nondescript things that people actually wanted but were not fun — facades of strip malls, that kind of thing. But his real joy was doing sculpture and actually building things. He was a good-looking guy, and he was a very charismatic guy, really smart. He was not interested in authority."

Geoff Outlaw, a fellow Stockbridge student and a friend of Arlo's since fourth grade, says that Ray had a childlike quality. "He was ten years younger than us even though he was older than us."

Director Arthur Penn would later describe him as "a dream spinner, but he was also a bullshit artist of magnitude."

Alice grew up in a middle-class home. Her mother came from a family of Russian Jewish immigrants; her father had been raised Irish Catholic. Alice demonstrated an interest in art and a flair for the dramatic at an early age. She started drawing at age seven. She had no palettes or paints, so she improvised. After school she would cover rolls of adding-machine tape with her doodles. Then, after dinner, she would show her family home movies: tapes reeled off on a miniature screen made out of an oatmeal box, to the accompaniment of her own stories.

Alice once said she was always in trouble as a girl, even spending some time in reform school. As she grew older, she developed a love of literature, especially the Beat poets. She once appeared in *Life* magazine at the side of poet Tuli Kupferberg. She went to Sarah Lawrence College on a scholarship, a fact about her life she once called "inconsistent and embarrassing." After leaving school she worked in New York for a time as a waitress. There she met Ray Brock, a man with similar interests and perspectives. They both enjoyed nature and the outdoors. Both were influenced by Jack Kerouac and the artists of the Beat Generation who sought an alternative to what they saw as stifling middle-class values. After a brief courtship they were married in a civil ceremony.

"The two of them together were very dynamic because they were both these strong personalities," Rick Robbins recalls. "When they had their fights it was hard, but when they were grooving together they were really energetic. Both artists, they just had something that attracted other people to them."

In 1962 Alice's mother, Mary Pelkey, was working as the registrar at the Stockbridge School, a private boarding school in Interlaken,

Massachusetts. Founded in 1949 by Hans Maeder, a thirty-nine-year-old German political refugee, the coeducational school offered a curriculum grounded in a liberal philosophy and emphasizing music and the arts. A number of the students there were children of well-known parents. Because the classes were small and the students were together day and night, the friendships they formed were more enduring than they might have been at a public high school with a graduating class of five hundred. The students also developed close relationships with some of the teachers, whom they addressed by their first names.

Through Mary Pelkey, Ray got a position at the Stockbridge School teaching architecture, and Alice became the librarian. They were among the youngest teachers at the institution. Their anti-Establishment, Beat philosophy resonated with the students, many of whom faced the looming threat of being sent against their will to fight a war in Vietnam. (U.S. troops in Vietnam totaled more than 15,000 by the end of 1963.)

"I met [the Brocks] when they were doing normal work pretending to be normal people at a very prestigious school," Arlo says. "They didn't fit in there at all, but all the kids loved them because they were different at a time when there was a real division between generations. So they came right between the two groups of people who were vying for power with each other. And they made life easier both for some of the staff at the school and some of the kids who were going there. But eventually they just got kicked out of there. They were just too different."

Alice, on the other hand, does not remember the Stockbridge School as "prestigious." "Hans Maeder would find people who were not teachers but they had a subject — they were biologists or something," she says. "He gave you a place to live. He collected a lot of oddballs. I was not a librarian, and nobody there was really a teacher. You can love your field, but that doesn't make you a teacher for a bunch of screwed-up kids. They were kids that probably got thrown out of public schools or had some problems in school or had parents who had enough money to get rid of them. Since it was a liberal, UN-ish kind of school, it was an interesting bunch of kids. They were bright. They had gotten in trouble probably. It wasn't a finishing school."

The Brocks, especially Ray, became hip surrogate parents for many of the students. Ray taught them carpentry and encouraged them to play music and "do their own thing."

"I got into things with them," he once told a reporter. "Whatever they were interested in I took an interest in, sports or just building things. They just needed to relate to someone older who was interested in them for a change."

Ray Brock teaches the art of carving to Rick Robbins, 1963.

James Broderick, the actor who would later portray Ray in the film *Alice's Restaurant*, spoke to a *Newsweek* reporter about the influence Ray had on the Stockbridge School students. "I didn't learn who Ray was from talking to him but from looking at the way the kids in the church reacted to me, with all the emotion a kid has for a folk hero. They would come up to me on the set and say, 'How can you possibly play Ray? He changed my life.'"

If Ray was the father figure, then Alice was naturally the mother figure, even though she was not much older than the students herself.

"It's surprising how young she was at that time," says Stockbridge alum Steve Elliot. "When you're fifteen, a woman of twenty-one or twenty-two seems so much older than you."

The Brocks worked at the Stockbridge School for only one academic season, but that was long enough to earn the friendship and loyalty of many of the students. One of these students was Arlo Guthrie.

"In a way, Woody taught us that what other people thought didn't make any difference."

— Arlo Guthrie

Brooklyn, 1947

Arlo Davy Guthrie was born July 10, 1947, with an impressive artistic pedigree. His maternal grandmother, Aliza Greenblatt, a Russian Jewish immigrant, wrote Yiddish poems and songs that are still performed by klezmer bands. She was a highly respected friend of most of the leading Yiddish writers of her day. Arlo's mother, Marjorie Mazia, was a professional dancer and, for eighteen years, Martha Graham's personal assistant. His father, Woody, was a folk musician who would achieve legendary status in Arlo's lifetime.

As Arlo would later write in his newsletter, the *Rolling Blunder Review,* "My parents were both very creative people and outstanding in their respective fields, which explains my life. My father notes that I screamed a lot and that I also banged on things. It became my mission in life."

Arlo's unusual name came from a book about a boy who had to collect firewood for his parents in a wagon. As a child, Marjorie had drawn a picture of the boy as she imagined him. She kept the picture. ("My mother saved everything," Arlo told Roger Dietz of *Acoustic Guitar*. "I have every ticket stub of every performance she went to from the fourth grade on, along with detailed commentary about each event.")

One day, when she was pregnant with Arlo, Marjorie was walking on the beach with Woody, who was pulling their three-year-old daughter, Cathy Ann, in a wagon. It suddenly struck Marjorie that her husband looked just like the picture she had drawn as a girl. Woody decided right then that if the baby was a boy he would be named Arlo. Marjorie was not as sure. She was afraid that her son might not like having such an uncommon name. They decided to give him the middle name "Davy" so he could use it if he didn't like his first name. "Arlo," incidentally, is the Spanish word for "barberry."

Decades later, in 1990, researchers Bruce Lansky and Barry Sinrod polled more than 75,000 people to find out what images they associated with a number of first names. Thanks to Arlo Guthrie, they found, "people picture 'Arlo' as a pot-smoking musical hippie."

Arlo's arrival into the world was bittersweet. The Guthries' first child, Cathy Ann, was tragically killed in a fire on her fourth birthday. Arlo was born five months later.

Woody Guthrie announced the birth of his son in a letter to the Guthries' nineteen-year-old babysitter, Natanya Neuman, by writing from the perspective of the newborn:

> Well, I done it. I jumped out of Marjorie's tummy down here at the Brooklyn Jewish Hospital at nine forty seven am on the am of the tenth of Julio nineteen forty seven this rough year. Weighed seven pounds and lost three ounces down there boxfighting with them baby basket kids and them folks that always come to see you after your stommick gets littler. My Mommy Marjorie tells me that I didn't cause her very much pains or scratches nor bruises neither one, nor no blood was lost by my Father Woody neither one, no hurt nurses, no kicked visitors. Nearly almost painless. I am calling myself Arlo, Arlo Guthrie, painless painless Arlo Guthrie. I am so painless that my Ma already wants to start all over again and track back to the same old spot and place where she found

me at and try to find her another one or two just about like me. That's how painless I am. You could feel of me all over here right this very minute in my crib and you couldn't feel no kind of pain, none, not no pains in me at all. And my Daddy is slowly getting painless which is really something to make me feel like I done moved Pikes Mountain over just a bit. Anyway, I was a breach baby. I come out feet first. But you know how jammed packed crowded and drove through these hospitals are these days, they've just not got enough room down there for you to jump out headfirst like you really want to.

Arlo was not an only child for long. His brother, Joady Ben (named after Tom Joad), was born in December 1948, and another sister, Nora Lee, was born a little over a year later. Being so close in age, the Guthrie children were playmates and carried their close relationship into adulthood. All three spent time with Alice and Ray at the church.

Perhaps because he worked at home writing songs, Woody involved himself in the care of the children, changing their diapers and taking them out to play, which was not necessarily expected of a man in the 1950s. But he never got over the loss of his beloved Cathy Ann. The colicky, fussy boy who was born just months after her death required more patience than Woody was always able to give. Within a month after Arlo's birth he wrote, "Today I slammed my door with hate and the wind blew back acrost little Arlo . . . and you cried all morning till I opened that same old door with love."

Although Joady bears a more striking resemblance to Woody, Arlo clearly had much in common with his father — most notably a musical talent that he revealed early on. Marjorie once described him in a letter to Woody as "a little version of you." When Arlo was only three, he played the harmonica and danced, imitating his father. Woody gave him the nickname "Dybbuk" or "Dyb" after he and Marjorie saw the Yiddish play *The Dybbuk*.

Arlo's home environment helped nurture his innate talent. When he was growing up, the Guthries' Coney Island home was often visited by professional dancers and musicians — the Weavers, Jack Elliot, Cisco Houston, Leadbelly — heroes to people like Ray Brock. To Arlo, they were just his parents' grown-up friends. In those days they mostly told little Arlo to go out and play.

Arlo's musical instruction came from his mother, not his father. Woody bought Arlo his first guitar, an $80 extravagance, but Marjorie taught him to play. She also made him take piano lessons. As Arlo tells it, he didn't like piano lessons and never learned to read music. He learned by listening and repeating. After his piano teacher played a piece of music on the page, he would say, "That sounds so pretty. Can you play it again?" With enough repetition, he would learn it by ear.

Arlo's mother, however, *could* read music. "She was Beethoven in a former life," he says. Marjorie told him that he would have to sit at the piano every day for an hour. It didn't matter if he played or not — he had to sit at the piano. Much to his mother's chagrin, Arlo would sit at the piano . . . and play the guitar. One day, during his enforced piano hour, he made what he calls "an amazing discovery": The C chord on the guitar was the same as the C chord on the piano. In fact, all the notes were the same. Pretty soon he was playing both instruments. He also learned by slowing recordings to half speed and playing along with them. Arlo liked to listen to the Everly Brothers, which he says impressed the girls more than traditional folk music did.

He started writing his own songs from the time he was little. "He would write songs late at night and early in the morning," Marjorie told a *Newsweek* reporter, "and whatever the hour he'd come running down the stairs yelling, 'Hey, Mom, listen to this. I got a new song!'"

Woody Guthrie, of course, was also a musical influence on Arlo. Arlo's first song, according to his mother, was a parody of Woody's "So Long, It's Been Good to Know You," with lyrics about a math test. But most of the younger Guthrie's appreciation for his father's music came second-hand. He was influenced by musicians who were influenced by his father — Woody's good friend Pete Seeger, whom Arlo calls "Uncle Pete," and people like Ramblin' Jack Elliot and Bob Dylan. (A British magazine once wrote, "Arlo Guthrie is Woody Guthrie's son. Bob Dylan only wishes he were.") Although it may seem strange that Woody did not have a more direct influence on his son's music, it was perfectly natural. People who appreciated Woody's music were always around. Woody himself, unfortunately, was not.

Arlo never saw his father perform. When he was just a toddler, Woody began to show the symptoms of a rare disorder known as Huntington's chorea, which strikes one in twenty thousand people. This degenerative hereditary disease results in dementia and the loss of bodily control. In the early stages, Woody's symptoms were mistaken for alcoholism or schizophrenia. Already an emotional man, he became prone to fits of violence. He was potentially dangerous to the family and impossible to live with. He and Marjorie separated and later divorced, and the family moved to Howard Beach, New York.

Marjorie began dating again right away. For a number of years she was involved with an auto mechanic named Tony Marra. When that didn't work out, she met and married Al Addeo, a carpenter. But her devotion to Woody never waned, even when he briefly remarried and his young wife, Anneke, had a daughter they named Lorina Lynn Guthrie. Marjorie was still dedicated to caring for Woody, who was hospitalized permanently when Arlo was six.

"I had father substitutes constantly coming into the house," Marjorie told author Joe Klein. "I needed the relationships, and I felt the children needed a man around the house. I'm not a person who can live without relationships. The beautiful thing is that all the father substitutes were people who loved Woody too."

Every few weekends the family visited the hospital or took Woody out for the day. On some of these visits Woody taught Arlo "a few things on the guitar," including, one memorable day, a verse to "This Land Is Your Land" that was usually left out of the version that appeared in patriotic songbooks:

> As I was walking
> I saw a sign there
> And on the sign it said "Private Property"
> But on the other side
> It didn't say nothing
> That side was made for you and me.

Woody was afraid that if he didn't teach the rebellious version to Arlo, it would be forgotten forever. Arlo calls it "my verse." It is a story he tells precisely because it was a rare moment of musical exchange between father and son. "You could still understand him, and he obviously

75

understood us," Arlo told author Joanna Powell. "He was interested in what was going on in our lives, in the everyday things. I didn't feel any extraordinary need to talk philosophically while he was sick. We didn't talk about rocket scientist stuff."

Sometimes, though, the visits must have been confusing and frightening for Arlo and his siblings, Joady and Nora. As Joe Klein wrote in *Woody Guthrie: A Life*:

> In general, Woody's Sunday-afternoon visits were difficult for the children. Howard Beach was a very conservative working-class neighborhood, and the Guthries were considered dangerously artsy and bizarre well before Marjorie's former husband began to show up, shaking and spluttering, often insisting on taking all his clothes off in the back yard and sometimes flying into noisy temper tantrums, ruining Sunday afternoons for the neighbors. "I guess the parents told the kids to kind of stay away from us," Arlo remembered, "which only made us more interesting to the kids. We weren't very popular in the neighborhood . . . but after a while, we began to realize that it wasn't Woody's fault and it wasn't ours — it was just that some people were narrow-minded and dumb. In a way, Woody taught us that what other people thought didn't make any difference."

Basically, Arlo says, this was his life, and not having another life to compare it to, it seemed normal. "I've been asked this a lot, so I've thought about it probably more than most people, but I still really don't have an answer. We just took life as we saw it every day . . . We thought that was fairly normal, and when I look back at it, you know, that's a lot more than some kids see their parents today."

In the 1950s, Woody's songs were copyrighted for the first time, and royalties began to come in, allowing Marjorie to send Arlo to private school beginning with the sixth grade. He went to Woodward School. In the summers he attended camp in Stockbridge, where his mother was a dance instructor. To those who knew him well, Arlo revealed a great sense of humor and a natural talent for mimicry, but he didn't make friends easily. He was shy and sensitive, and the other boys teased him because he was bad at sports. He responded by withdrawing into his own world, going off into the woods, building hideouts, and making up stories.

One of his favorite toys, according to Marjorie, was a devil puppet she had given him. One summer during a volleyball game, he played so badly that a fellow camper decided to get even by breaking the puppet. When Arlo discovered the broken toy, he calmly went into the other boy's tent and tore everything apart.

Arlo returned to the same summer camp for five years, though, and slowly made friends with the counselors and a few kids who liked his guitar playing and weren't as concerned with sports. At the end of his last summer there he was given the award for the camper who had shown the most all-around improvement. As Marjorie recalled, "The entire camp broke into a tremendous roar. Arlo couldn't stop grinning."

He was never a serious student. He liked art and music and discussing ideas, but he was not too interested in details. His eighth grade social studies teacher, Mrs. Greenstein, reported that Arlo's "understanding of social problems indicates his ability to empathize with people and analyze situations with intelligent judgment. His careless work habits deter him from presenting himself at his true level in written work. He employs research skills in a superficial manner, and only occasionally completes an assigned task." His music teacher, Miss Mayo, said, "Arlo is talented musically, but needs a great deal of help and guidance in self-discipline. He is a 'natural' musician, but tends to fool around, hit wrong notes, and to just get by with what comes easily. In this last year, though, he has shown amazing growth in poise and in technique in guitar-playing. He still hasn't enough self-discipline to play in an orchestra. He is definitely a solo player, so far, at least."

Although he never did become much of a scholar, things improved socially when he went to the Stockbridge School. There he found friends who appreciated his musical ability, imagination, and unique outlook on life. Arlo kept on building cabins in the woods, but this time his friends joined in. As he told the *New Yorker* in 1968, "We built a whole community up there, with a constitution that had only one rule: You can't build your cabin in sight of anyone else's. Everyone was very beautiful about the whole scene. I built four cabins, half buried in the ground, and camouflaged, waterproof, snowproof. We had stoves and the whole thing.

One cabin was one and a half stories. It was like an outlet from school — an exit. Any school is like a prison. I've always had to find a way to fit in but always leave a back door open."

Paul Kleinwald remembers Arlo as a creative young man with a wonderful sense of humor. "In high school, he used to draw these little figures — cartoon figures — and the series would go on. Every once in a while he'd come up with a new adventure in the series. He had good wit and good timing. Lord knows there are people who play musical instruments better than he does, and there are people who sing a hell of a lot better than he does. He just has a talent and an inner warmth and way of communicating with people. He's been very successful because of his wonderful sense of humor, timing, his appreciation for music, and his ability to relate on a personal level to his audience."

Arlo's interest in music was already apparent. In fact, there was a legend at the school that they had to take his guitar away so he would study.

"He wasn't popular like Joe College," says fellow alumnus Steve Elliot, "but everybody was fond of him. He was so accomplished at such a young age. When he'd perform with us, and talk with us, he had a charm he could exude."

Alice does not remember Arlo as shy at all. "He was right in there with the rest of the kids," she says, clearly surprised at the suggestion. Arlo's class, the class of 1965, was especially close knit and left its mark on the school. When Arlo was in the tenth grade, the year the Brocks were employed at Stockbridge, half the class spent an entire week writing little messages that said "Sophomores rule." One night, as everyone else slept, they snuck around the school and stuck them everywhere — on chairs, on people's pillows, on notebooks, anything they could think of.

"Three or four years later I still found some of these notes around," Paul Kleinwald recalls with a laugh.

The kids also had a touch of rebellion about them. The school had a rule that boys had to wear jackets and ties. Thin ties and tight lapels were in fashion then. So the students would go to the Goodwill store in Pittsfield and buy old double-breasted suits and big wide ties, which, while in accordance with the rules, looked odd instead of neat. The school changed the rules after that.

Although Alice and Ray Brock had already purchased the church at this point, they had not yet moved in and had few guests as they began renovating. Even if he had wanted to go, Arlo says, he did not have the freedom to visit the Brocks' church often in the early days.

"I only went over there in the summer, in the first summer, and spent a few weeks, just to visit and see what they were doing there," he says. "I didn't have a car. I was a kid in school. In the school I was going to, you couldn't leave anytime you wanted to. You were really locked in there for the duration. So on holidays or something we'd go over there to see what was going on, but it was never a permanent thing."

He got closer to the Brocks shortly thereafter when the couple worked at a youth hostel on Martha's Vineyard. Arlo was one of the young people who followed them there.

"We spent a good portion of the summer of '63, me and my brother, with Ray and Alice at the youth hostel," Arlo remembers. "That's where we really played music every day. Rick Robbins was playing, my brother was there, a couple of other people were there . . . Liza Condon, who was Eddie Condon's daughter. Ray and Alice had connections to New York. And that's when I really became friends with them. So we just basically partied our way through the summer of '63. We'd make incredible batches of brandy Alexanders, go to the beach and play all day, and go look for places to play at night with whoever was coming through. There was a whole sort of music scene on the Vineyard that tied to New York, and the connection was through Ray and Alice. They were more than just two people who had a church, and they were more than just two teachers I had met."

Arlo became serious about his own musical career around this time. He gave his first public concert at age thirteen, performing his father's songs in Greenwich Village.

"At first they probably hired me because they thought I would be a draw, being that I was Woody's son," Arlo once said. "And I did. But I don't think people would have kept coming back for that."

What they did come back for was Arlo's unique blend of tradition and irreverence. They came not only to hear his songs but to enjoy his sense of humor. Arlo played songs like Woody's "Roll On, Columbia," but instead of doing it straight, he turned it into a mock commercial for a deodorant.

Arlo admits that at first he was "frightened beyond belief" to face an audience, but eventually he found that performing could give him a new way to relate to people. As his manager, Harold Leventhal, told *Newsweek*, "Arlo has difficulty with personal relationships, but in a concert situation that personal relationship doesn't exist. A lot of people who can't communicate with one person find a tremendous liberation onstage."

Arlo himself explained it to author Kathy Cronkite this way: "My stage personality allows me to be more receptive to a greater number of people than my offstage personality, which requires that I get into fewer people . . . It always impressed me that people thought I was the same onstage and off, because I didn't feel the same. How can you be the same? How can you talk to five thousand people the same as you'd talk to two? You can't. You're stupid if you think you can, if you attempt it. But that doesn't mean you can't be just as intimate with five thousand people as you can with two. You just have to find a different mode to do it in."

After graduating from Stockbridge, he spent the summer in Europe busking and playing in clubs. When he returned to the States, he went to what he called "the closest college that would take me" — Rocky Mountain College in Billings, Montana. Not surprisingly, given his academic prowess, his stay at the college was brief; he lasted only six weeks. "They were uptight about long hair and me," he once said. He also told a reporter he'd decided to leave college when he heard Bob Dylan's "Positively Fourth Street" on the radio. "I said, 'My God. That's incredible that they're playing this song on the radio.' It was enough to make me leave college, although it wasn't the only thing."

With his academic career finished and his musical career just beginning, Arlo found his way back to the Berkshires whenever he could to visit his friends in the Brocks' church-home.

"Alice didn't live in the restaurant, she lived in the church nearby the restaurant with her husband Ray and Facha the dog . . ."

—Arlo Guthrie
"Alice's Restaurant"

Housatonic, 1963

he old Trinity Church was not the kind of home that you could just move into. It had been designed for one purpose, to hold religious services on Sunday. There were no bathrooms, no kitchens, no bedrooms. There was a huge arched sanctuary with a few chestnut pews still in place. On either side of the altar were two small rooms — one where the minister put on his church vestments, the other a sewing room and later a storage room for books. A rickety ladder in the bell tower led up to a series of small landings. At the top was, of course, the bell, with a rope that hung all the way down to the ground floor.

"We didn't have any money at all," Alice recalls. "My mother went to the bank to see if she could get a mortgage to make it habitable. She had good credit, so they gave one to her. And so Ray went up there and started to add those things one would like to have — bathrooms, heat, insulation. There was no way we were going to heat that whole place. So we just lived in the tower. Of course, we didn't live like other people. We didn't require the accoutrements other people needed."

Early guests at the church had a view of the stars when they stayed in the room at the top of the bell tower. You could see through the beams to the outside. There was an electric blanket on the bed, and guests would run up and turn it on, then go back downstairs while it warmed up. After a few minutes they would run back up and jump into the bed.

The first thing Ray did was to build a series of floors in the once-hollow structure of the bell tower. On the ground floor was the kitchen; above that, the bathroom and bedrooms with "a bed and a chair and some nails to hang your clothes on. It was not like we had wall-to-wall carpeting," Alice says.

PAUL KLEINWALD

Ray Brock working in the rafters of the church, around 1963.

When Rick Robbins first visited the church, Ray had just finished single-handedly hauling a bathtub up to the second level of the bell tower. "Taking this church and converting it into a house was pure Ray. It was typical," Rick says. "It was this huge challenge of taking this building that was not designed as a house. It was such a beautiful building. And the idea of living in a space that big — if you have this huge room like a gymnasium, you can set up all your stuff. Alice had her easels up — she was doing paintings. Ray was doing sculpture."

What the Brocks lacked in funds they more than made up for in creativity. The chestnut pews became kitchen cabinets and banisters for the stairs. Although the stained-glass windows were beautiful, they didn't let in much light. So the Brocks took out the large arched doorway in the bell tower and replaced it with a window. Alice wanted an Oriental rug for the kitchen, but since she could not afford one, she painted the kitchen floor with polka dots instead.

"It was really a beautiful building," Arlo says. "What they had done to the building was spectacular. They were both very artistic people, and they had created a place that just felt incredibly different, almost like being on a ship. Ray had made these stairways that went up through the bell tower that were half ladder and half stairs. They had created this incredible little place and created all these little nooks and crannies that went up through each room. Each space was really small and compact. Instead of having dressers, there would be shelving and drawer space under a bed like you would see on a ship or in a place where space was really tight. You don't have a lot, but you still have to have all the stuff. They had these really tiny bedrooms with windows that looked out from the bell tower. In those days they didn't have the chimney that's there now and the fireplace to secure it, so when you went up there in the room and the wind started blowing, you could have a glass half full of water and it would spill just sitting there. It would move."

As a classically trained architect, Ray was careful to maintain the architectural integrity of the Gothic building. When he put in a doorway to close off the sanctuary so he wouldn't have to heat it, he framed it as a classic Gothic arch. Work on the building was a job, hobby, social activity, and educational tool all rolled into one. Ray taught the young men from the school how to construct a Gothic arch and how to mix the kind of plaster that had been used in the original construction of the building a century earlier.

The group also used their construction skills renovating barns and building ships. Motorcycle racing was another hobby. They made up names for their "clubs" based on the name of the old church. There was the Trinity Heavy Duty Construction Company and the Trinity Racing Association. The racing association had its own symbol, a red trinitarian triangle with an infinity sign in the center.

For the recent Stockbridge School graduates, many of whom were drifting, unsure of what to do next, the church was a kind of clubhouse or headquarters where they could continue the friendships they had formed at school.

"We were kids, so we had all these conflicts with our parents being so straight. We wanted to get away from the Establishment," Rick Robbins says. "We wanted to just drop out and not be part of selling out or the corporate world. At the time we were just dreaming, but it was a great dream, and for a short time there was a lot of magic happening through that building."

The church was a place where the kids could discuss with adults matters that they might not want to talk about with Mom and Dad, and do things their parents wouldn't necessarily approve of. Drugs — marijuana and psychedelics — were common, although Alice quips that she spends more on prescription drugs today than she ever did on drugs in the '60s.

"A lot of kids lived with us," she says. "The parents thought it was great because we were teachers. They'd never even met us, but we were teachers, so we must have been responsible adults. So if we were taking their kids and feeding them and giving them a place to sleep, that was a good deal. There were clean sheets on the beds. The dishes were washed. We had a phone. They knew where the kids were. There were no parents screaming that we had taken their kids away. They were glad they knew where their kids were."

Tom Hebner, whose son Tommy spent time at the church, has nothing but praise for the Brocks and their friends. "Ray Brock was really the inspiration behind the whole thing at the church. He was a good man. People said that people just smoked dope up there, but he liked people, and he just did things that inspired people. He helped people every way he could. And he always had people at that church. All kinds of people. He was a wonderful man, I always thought. Alice we didn't know personally, but our son knew her."

"She was a fine personality," adds his wife, Frances.

"At that era we were not in that same position that the young people were," Tom Hebner says good-naturedly. "We were in what you call the generation gap."

The friends didn't just spend time together in the confines of the church. They raced their motorcycles at the Hebners' farm, among other places. Tom Hebner remembers them singing a silly song while they raced: "I don't want a pickle, just want to ride on my motorsickle." Years later he heard the song again. "I heard the song on television one night when we were in Florida. Tommy used to come home and he'd be singing this song because they'd be practicing this at the church, him and Ray Brock and Arlo. I never realized that was a real song."

The kitchen on the first floor of the bell tower. Left to right: Geoff Outlaw, Tigger Outlaw, Alice Brock, Arlo Guthrie, Caroly Davis, Ray Brock.

Alice, meanwhile, planted flowers and a vegetable garden behind the church. As she tilled the soil, she turned up glassy blue rocks — slag from the old iron furnace. The garden was a delight for a city girl like Alice: "You plant the seeds and free food comes up!"

Spaghetti was a common meal for the numerous house guests. It was inexpensive and could be dressed up with whatever vegetables came from the garden. Concocting great meals on limited resources was a skill Alice had picked up intuitively as a child.

"Somehow both my parents were obsessed with food," she wrote in her book *My Life as a Restaurant*. "My mother's obsession probably came from a lack of food — she came from a poor Russian immigrant family . . . Creative cooking was the result of having to make something out of nothing. When you're poor, a chicken foot can present a lot of possibilities . . . My father was not concerned with cost as much as quality."

Some kids stayed at the old church for long periods of time; others just stopped in for one of Alice's home-cooked meals. There were sometimes as many as fifteen young people there at one time, using the bedrooms or sleeping on the floor in the sanctuary in warm weather.

"Everyone played guitar," Alice recalls. "We didn't have a television or all that stuff. We just sat around and ate lots of spaghetti. People would come and go. The word gets out in the underground. If you're out there, you can always stay there with Alice and Ray and she'll do your laundry. You'll have a place to sleep and shower. People would just appear. They'd be friends of friends of friends. It was all very trusting. It's almost inconceivable. We were so innocent, but we could be. People's first thought wasn't how they could screw you. We were working for a better world. We had a positive and loving point of view. We believed everyone should be themselves and be accepted. People should have their own thoughts and form their own opinions. So we attracted an interesting bunch."

Arlo once said the period of trust lasted "about eight months, where you could look somebody in the eye across the street and if he sorta looked like he was outta the mainstream, you could trust him."

They didn't look that way to the neighbors. The Berkshires at that time resembled nothing so much as the paintings of famous Stockbridge artist Norman Rockwell, or at least it aspired to look that way. Some colonial villages in the area had barely changed over the decades. Woodstock was several years away, and most of the residents of the former Van Deusenville had never seen young people who looked like these. They would have been a curious enough sight in any case, but they were also living in a church. The Brocks made friends with a few of the neighbors. Mary Sachs, despite her feelings about the new environment at her church, remembers Alice fondly. She says they used to take walks and talk about their common interest in gardening. Even so, the majority of the neighbors simply had no idea what to make of them.

Paul Kleinwald remembers one particular dispute with the neighbors very well. Apparently Ray had had a lot of trouble with a local dog officer who lived around the corner. The officer claimed Ray's dog was chasing deer. Ray suspected this was not true because the dog was small and a little lame. Eventually, however, the officer shot the dog.

"It was pretty sad," Paul says. "I went over with another fellow and we picked up the dog in a plastic bag. That was kind of hard."

"We were freaks. We were total freaks," Alice says. "We were not welcome. First of all, we were scary because we had long hair and I didn't wear a brassiere. And we were not wacky. Ray used to wear a corduroy suit and a little necktie. He had hair that went past his ears or something. We were from New York, and who the hell were we to live in a church?

Ray would be in there, sawing and hammering, and he'd sit out on the steps and drink some beers. Sitting on the steps of the church and drinking beers! I used to sunbathe out there in a bikini. It was my front yard, but I was on the front steps of a church. People came by, they yelled, they honked. There was no welcome wagon. Word got out that there were beatniks in the church, and people would come and walk right in. 'I'm just here to see the freaks.' They didn't acknowledge us as humans, and they didn't acknowledge that as our home. People wouldn't walk into someone's home.

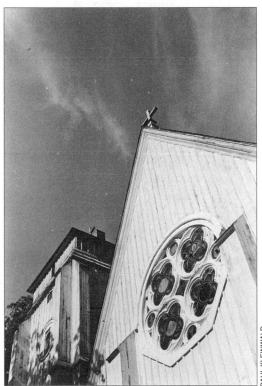

Paul Kleinwald's artistic vision of the church.

I hate to tell you what Ray said to them. They had never seen anything like it. There were an awful lot of people in the Berkshires who were sure that whole movement in the sixties, all those protests and all those sit-ins and be-ins and demonstrations, were all because of Alice and Ray at the church. Anybody whose kid dropped out of school, it was our fault."

Although many people believe the church was a hippie commune where the kids did nothing but paint their faces, smoke pot, and dance all day, the young people all had their own places to live. The Brocks were just, as one person put it, "delightfully social," and their home would have been a center of activity whether it was a church or a garage.

"Ray and Alice bought a great building," Rick Robbins says. "The years at the church, there were a lot of interesting people that arrived there out of curiosity. They were always welcome to come, in the tradition of Woody Guthrie and the Guthrie family. They picked up strays all the time. They would see everybody equally. Ray would always say, 'Come on up.' We'd go skiing. We'd do normal stuff. We weren't sitting around just doing nothing."

There might not always have been a "scene happening" at the church, but occasionally they did have big parties, like the feast they planned for Thanksgiving, 1965.

"We'd never heard of a dump closed on Thanksgiving before . . ."

— Arlo Guthrie
"Alice's Restaurant"

Housatonic, Thanksgiving, 1965

T hanksgiving was observed by the Episcopal Church before it was officially recognized in all of the United States. It wasn't until 1863 — three years before the wooden Trinity Church was built — that President Abraham Lincoln proclaimed the last Thursday in November as a day to give thanks. Experts disagree on the ultimate origin of the holiday in America, but they do agree that the idea of a feast of Thanksgiving was not born in this country.

Greeks and Romans paid homage to the gods of agriculture. Anglo-Saxons celebrated Lammas and Harvest Home long before the Pilgrims arrived on our shores and had their own celebration of the harvest before the long cold winter. Some historians call December 4, 1619, our first Thanksgiving. On that date English settlers observed a religious day of thanks.

Others claim that the first Thanksgiving feast actually took place in El Paso, Texas, in 1598. According to El Paso legend, Don Juan de Onate

Alice Brock in the church kitchen. This mess was staged for the movie Alice's Restaurant but was probably similar to the dishes she faced on Thanksgiving, 1965.

landed on the banks of the Rio Grande on April 20 of that year. Ten days later he and his crew shared a feast of thanksgiving with Native Americans.

The Schwenkfeers of Pennsylvania Dutch country hold a feast of thanksgiving on September 24. Canadian Thanksgiving is the second Monday in October. But most of us think of the first Thanksgiving as the one that took place in Plymouth in 1621.

Whatever its origin, for Alice and Ray, Thanksgiving was an excuse to have friends over. They had a lot of friends, old friends from New York and students who had graduated from the Stockbridge School. Even those who were away at college returned to the area for Thanksgiving break. All in all there would be quite a gathering for Alice's famous cuisine.

Getting the church set up for the dinner was no small task. Normally during the colder months, the former sanctuary was closed off because it was too difficult and expensive to heat, but for this special occasion they opened it up. To make sure it would be warm enough, Ray had to fire up Fanny Bostwick's big coal stoves in the basement three days in advance.

The church was pretty livable by now, but the Brocks were still working on it. Since they rarely used the sanctuary in cold weather, they had piled up garbage in the corner. "That big room had piles and piles of trash," Alice says. "It wasn't chicken bones and empty tin cans; it was building debris or piles of lumber. There was lots of plaster and old stuff."

Of course it would have to be moved before the guests arrived for dinner. Alice was cooking the turkey. Ray was shoveling coal. So a couple of friends who were staying with them offered to haul the garbage away.

By 1965, Arlo was traveling and playing music in coffeehouses. His friend Rick Robbins, a fellow musician, was traveling with him. "Harold Leventhal had set up a bunch of gigs for Arlo, and I was following along," Rick says. "Arlo had the gigs. I wasn't making any money. So we traveled around up and down the East Coast. Whenever we were around, we'd go to the church. I think we were just there at Thanksgiving by accident. We were on our way back from Chicago or something. We stopped there. The garbage had to be taken out, and Arlo was at the wheel."

They loaded the lumber, plaster, boxes, bottles, papers, junk mail, and even an old sofa into the back of a red VW microbus with a Trinity Racing Association triangle on the side and made their way to the Great Barrington dump. The dump was closed for Thanksgiving, but Arlo remembered a place near the summer camp he'd attended as a kid. It had its own, unofficial dump in a small gully. There the two young men threw the garbage.

"People think we dumped the garbage over this pristine hillside," Rick says, "but it was a place where a lot of people were already dumping garbage. There are a lot of misconceptions. Some people actually think we were protesting the war or something."

Then, without a second thought, they went back to the church. The dinner was an event. Alice had decorated the sanctuary and put tables up by the altar. Ray was wearing a top hat. There was food aplenty, some made by Alice, some brought by guests. Wine flowed freely, and even Facha the dog gorged on the bountiful table scraps.

CLEMENS KALISCHER

There was only one hitch. Someone had seen the two young men in the act of littering and reported it to the police. "Of course they had long hair and they were driving this kind of crazy Volkswagen bus, wearing bell-bottoms and wild colors and hats and stuff," Alice says ruefully. "They called the police."

It fell to Stockbridge police chief William J. Obanhein to figure out who the culprits were. Known as Bill to his friends — but never as

Obie — William Obanhein was born in 1924 in Stockbridge. Except for a stint in the Navy, when he served in Okinawa and on the *USS Arkansas* during the invasion of Normandy, he was a lifelong resident of the town. He graduated in 1943 from Williams High School and worked at General Electric before joining the police force in 1951. He was promoted to police chief in 1958 when the former chief died.

A big, broad-shouldered man with a gruff voice, Obanhein was an old-fashioned small-town cop, the kind who knew everyone in the town. Despite his imposing size, he was a gentle man who used his own judgment to enforce the law, based on what he knew of the people in his community. He drove people home when they were tipsy. A member of St. Joseph's Church, he once helped a rebellious kid find religion instead of getting into trouble. He served as dog officer for many years and once spent a whole night in a swamp searching for a lost dog. When dogs killed a cow on a local farm, he said that it couldn't have been Stockbridge dogs that committed the crime. "I know every one of them," he said. "Those were Lee dogs."

Like many in Stockbridge, he twice posed for the artist Norman Rockwell. He appears in a 1957 black-and-white drawing for the Massachusetts Mutual Life Insurance Company, part of a series of advertisements focusing on the values of the American family. In 1968 he was featured in an advertisement for Goodwill Industries.

On Thanksgiving Day, 1965, Bill Obanhein spent "a very disagreeable two hours" sifting through the pile of junk from the church. He finally came across some mail addressed to Ray Brock. He took photographs of the junk — black and white, not color. When they'd been developed, he marked them, not with circles and arrows, but with the words PROSPECT HILL RUBBISH DUMPING FILE UNDER GUTHRIE AND ROBBINS 11/26/65.

He called the church, where Ray, Alice, Arlo, Rick, and a few other friends were sitting at the kitchen table drinking coffee. Alice answered the phone.

"Someone dumped this garbage. I think it's your garbage. It's got your name all over it," Chief Obanhein said.

The chief could hear Alice through the muffled telephone asking the youths where they'd dumped the stuff. They told her. She muttered, "I'm going to kill you guys." Then, to the police chief, she said, "As a matter of fact they did do it, and they're going to hear about it from me."

"Well, I want them to hear about it from me," he said. "So will you have them go down to the police station?"

The nonconformist teenagers with their don't-trust-anyone-over-thirty attitude were trouble waiting to happen, but Chief Obanhein figured they were probably good kids underneath it all. So he wanted to scare them so they wouldn't cause any more problems for the community, and he hoped to make an example of them. They were arrested. Although he did not handcuff them, he did put them in a jail cell, a dreary, green-painted room with chicken wire on the window, a metal cot, and no seat on the toilet. Alice had to bail them out, and she was not happy about it. She yelled at the chief. He told her that if she didn't stop the verbal abuse, he'd arrest her too. So she stopped yelling, posted bail, and took the litterbugs home.

The collective memories of the rest of the day are fuzzy. Some remember Arlo coming back and starting to write a song that very night about his adventure, with everyone contributing their own verses. Some say it happened much later, or maybe much earlier. Some say that, frankly, they don't remember the decade that well, much less November 26, 1965.

What is clear is that the original lyrics, lost forever in time, would not have been as good-natured as those that appear on the album. It took Arlo some time to tap into the humor of the situation. At first, he says, "it was devastating" being arrested.

"We were very, very angry at Officer Obanhein, whom we didn't know," Alice once said. "We just met him that one time. But we used to sit around sometimes at the church and play music and crack jokes and laugh about how someday we were going to run him over or bury him in a pile of garbage. All these plans for revenge for a fifty-dollar fine."

In any case, "Alice's Restaurant" was not penned in one sitting. It began as a bed of music that a group of friends could invent silly verses for, and over the course of the year it slowly evolved into something much more structured as events continued to happen that appealed to Arlo's sense of the absurd.

"I wrote the song as a lark, really," Arlo told reporter Russell Hall. "We sat around laughing about the song, thinking it was stupid, but as time went on, other things started to happen. We had to go to court, we had to do this and that, and eventually I had to go down to New York to

REPRODUCED BY PERMISSION OF THE NORMAN ROCKWELL FAMILY TRUST

William Obanhein appeared in this 1957 Norman Rockwell illustration, which appeared in an ad for the Massachusetts Mutual Life Insurance Company.

deal with the draft board. And I kept incorporating all these things into what eventually became a monologue, using one of the verses to tie it all together."

Arlo and Rick Robbins appeared in Lee District Court before Special Justice James E. Hannon. Justice Hannon was born in Brockton, Massachusetts, two days before Christmas in 1909. He was blind in one eye at birth and lost the sight in his other eye at age eight. Despite his

REPRODUCED BY PERMISSION OF THE BERKSHIRE EAGLE

Youths Ordered To Clean Up Rubbish Mess

LEE – Because they couldn't find a dump space open in Great Barrington, two youths threw a load of refuse down a Stockbridge hillside on Thanksgiving Day.

Saturday, Richard J. Robbins, 19, of Poughkeepsie, N.Y., and Arlo Guthrie, 18, of Howard Beach, N.Y., each paid a fine of $25 in Lee District Court after pleading guilty of illegally disposing of rubbish. Special Justice James E. Hannon ordered the youths to remove all the rubbish. They did so Saturday afternoon, following a heavy rain.

Police Chief William J. Obanhein of Stockbridge said later the youths found dragging the junk up the hillside much harder than throwing it down. He said he hoped their case would be an example to others who are careless about disposal of rubbish.

The junk included a divan, plus nearly enough bottles, garbage, papers and boxes to fill their Volkswagon bus.

"The stuff would take up at least half of a goodsized pickup truck," Chief Obanhein said.

The rubbish was thrown into the Nelson Foote Sr. property on Prospect Street, a residential section of Stockbridge consisting largely of estates on the hill across from Indian Hill School.

Chief Obanhein told the court he spent "a very disagreeable two hours" looking through the rubbish before finding a clue to who had thrown it down there. He finally found a scrap of paper bearing the name of a Great Barrington man. Subsequent investigation indicated Robbins and Guthrie had been visiting the Great Barrington man and had agreed to cart away the rubbish for him. They told the court that, when they found the Barrington dump closed, they drove around and then disposed of the junk by tossing it over the Stockbridge hillside.

blindness, he graduated with honors from Boston University in 1933 and two years later earned his law degree there — magna cum laude, the first time in four years that a law student had graduated from BU with such a high rank. He moved to Lee in 1935 and opened a law practice in the same building as his brother, a dentist. He later served in Berkshire District Court and was named special justice of the court of Lee in 1960. John J. Dwyer, who withdrew his name from consideration in favor of Hannon, later described the judge as having "a keen mind, a distinguished educational background, a sense of fairness to all parties, and a compassionate concern for the problems of the less fortunate."

Arlo Guthrie and Rick Robbins were docket numbers 37577 and 37578 respectively. Other cases before the judge that day included speeding and failure to stop at a stop sign. Bill Obanhein, the complainant, showed up in court with the photographic evidence, which the judge could obviously not consider. In any case, the young men did not dispute the charges. They pleaded guilty and were fined $25 each (the average traffic violation commanded a fine of $5 to $10) and ordered to pick up the garbage, which they did the following

Saturday afternoon, after a heavy rain.

"We picked up a lot more than we originally put down there," Rick says. "Just like the song says."

Bill Obanhein told the *Berkshire Eagle* he hoped the case would be an example to others who were careless about the disposal of their rubbish.

Besides his littering arrest, which served as the foundation for Arlo's famous song, another event that captured his imagination was Alice's plan to open a restaurant. The chorus "You can get anything you want at Alice's restaurant" was not intended to be a commercial jingle, and the restaurant, of course, has little to do with the rest of the tale. Even Alice isn't sure how she ended up in the song.

"I never had a commercial on the radio. I couldn't afford that." she says. "He didn't write it for me. Alice's Restaurant . . . who knows how that creative mind works. He does have a fantastic mind, and he'll put things together that you never thought of, but once he's done it you say 'Oh, right!' He has a good imagination for those kinds of things. He had a passion. Some of those kids didn't have a particular passion like that. Some were photographers, some were artists, some were always trying to play the guitar or the banjo or the autoharp or something, and some were just out there. But that was his passion, and so he worked at it pretty much all the time."

"Alice's Restaurant" was, in fact, part of a trilogy of story-songs. There was one about how Lyndon Johnson devised his defense plan for America, another about how the song was a plot to overthrow the world, and finally the song that evolved out of the garbage-dumping arrest. It went through a number of incarnations before it became the song a generation knows and loves. Each story retained one common denominator, the chorus about Alice and the restaurant. The premise of the "Alice" prototype was: Before you know it, the whole world will be singing "Alice's Restaurant," so the sooner you learn the chorus, the better off you'll be. No one could have predicted how accurate that statement would be.

Alice did open her restaurant. By then the pressures of being an "Earth Mother"— as the press dubbed her — were taking their toll. Alice enjoyed the company of the people she still calls her "family," but she was the one making the spaghetti, putting clean sheets on the beds, and making sure there were clean towels in the bathroom.

"There were times when Alice would get completely frustrated with the number of people who were around," Rick says. "It didn't seem like a lot, but it was more than we realized. Friends would come by. Ray would always say, 'Come on up, stay,' and Alice would end up cooking for everybody and then wound up cleaning up for everybody."

There were other problems in the marriage. Ray was beginning to drink more heavily, and Alice, who had married at a relatively young age, was beginning to yearn for an identity of her own.

"As Alice matured and Ray didn't, it caused a lot of problems for her," says Steve Elliot. "She felt like she was carrying the load."

So when Mary Pelkey called Alice and told her there was a luncheonette called Maluphy's Restaurant for sale in Stockbridge, down a little alley between Nejaime's grocery store and Kempton's Insurance, Alice decided to take a look. After all, people always raved about her cooking. Maybe having a business of her own would give her some independence.

"People always ask me why I ever opened a restaurant in the first place," she wrote in *My Life as a Restaurant*. "I think a lot of people who are interested in food fantasize about having a restaurant. I never did. I was twenty-five, married, and crazy. I was a captive in a situation I had very little control over other than the role of cook and nag — being a hippie housewife was not satisfying. I had a world of fantasies; none included a restaurant, but all were based on the assumption that I would be my own person, on my own trip."

For a little while she enjoyed the creative act of inventing a menu from scratch and decorating the hole-in-the-wall with her own homey touches. She hung old-fashioned kitchen utensils and wooden decorations on the walls. (She still has most of them. They now grace the walls of the kitchen in her Cape Cod home.) As the song says, "Alice's Restaurant" was never the name of a restaurant. Her place in Stockbridge was called the Back Room Rest, and it was a success. It was frequented by famous actors from the Berkshire Playhouse, including Dustin Hoffman, Gene Hackman, and Anne Bancroft.

Reverend Middleton's daughter, Pam, was a waitress at the historic Red Lion Inn at the time. She remembers that the staff of the pricey restaurant bought their lunches at Alice's place. "There wasn't any better food anywhere. The way she cooked was the way you cook today. It wasn't the way people cooked in 1969. She's a fabulous cook. There isn't anyone better."

Unfortunately, running a restaurant did not provide Alice with the freedom she craved. Far from it. She was there from five or six in the morning to late at night, cooking, washing dishes, and doing the books, and things were still stressful at home. The dynamic at the church was changing. She was overworked and tired of taking care of everyone. Finally, about a year after she had opened the restaurant, Alice had had enough.

"I dragged my body in through the door and freaked out," she wrote. "I felt that instead of owning it, it owned me. The plates were out to get me, the pots were planning an attack, the stove was laughing at me. I had a terrible urge to smash everything. I telephoned Eastern Airlines and booked myself on the midnight flight to Puerto Rico. I emptied the cash box, gave away all the food . . . It was a wonderful restaurant. It was a success. I ran it for one year. It turned me into a madwoman. I made enemies of old friends, I broke up with my husband, I left my home. I had actually broken free and become my own person."

And then, as Alice and Ray's marriage was dissolving and the restaurant was closed, "Alice's Restaurant," the song by Arlo Guthrie, became very famous indeed.

"This song is called Alice's Restaurant. It's about Alice and the restaurant . . ."

— Arlo Guthrie
"Alice's Restaurant"

New York City, 1967

Commenting on the song "Alice's Restaurant," critic Robin Wood wrote: "Guthrie's narrative gives the deceptive impression of rambling inconsequentially, with its incessantly reiterated guitar tune, up to the point where he is asked at the draft interview, 'Kid, have you ever been arrested?' At which moment everything clicks neatly into place and, to point this, the accompaniment pauses for the first time in nearly fifteen minutes. It's a magical moment."

The song had been in the works for some time, but Arlo didn't discover the punch line until he was called to face the draft board. In reality, it was not the littering arrest that kept Arlo out of Vietnam. While the song implies this, it does not actually *say* that his deferment was a direct result of his being a litterbug. What it says is what really happened: Arlo and a friend were arrested for littering, the officer in charge took photographs of the crime scene, and the court was presided over by a blind judge. Later, when he went in for his army physical, he was asked if he had ever been arrested.

In 1966 Arlo registered as a conscientious objector. His letter to the draft board, printed in the 1969 *This Is the Arlo Guthrie Book,* read:

March 8, 1966

Throughout all of my life I have been learning and living by a love for people. I have grown to believe and depend upon a way of life, which has been created by my own life up till now. This way of life is also a reason for my existence. I am living because I have a reason to live, a job to do, a purpose in life. This purpose is to love people, and work with people so that we may all lead better lives, so that we can all love each other, so that we can learn from each other, and create a world where people do not grow hungry, where men are really free and where men are not hampered by fear, ignorance and war.

I do not believe that war is a means to attain good, nor that it creates love or respect for something good. I do not believe that today, anyone can win a war. Everyone involved can only lose. We can only defeat our own purpose.

There are many people all over the world that feel like I do. They are of all races and of all religions and in many cases a God is part of their belief.

My God is the love that people have for one another and this love is what I have devoted my life to, I want to see it grow until all war, hatred, fear and ignorance have disappeared from the earth. By going to war I am going against my basis for living. This is why I can not go to war.

Thank you,
Arlo Guthrie

The letter did not have the desired effect: Arlo was classified 1-A. The truth is that he was not disqualified for the draft at all. His number simply never came up.

"As far as the draft and all that, they do ask if you've ever been arrested, and for what," Alice says. "That's not how he got out of the draft, but I'm sure the whole thing struck him as kind of crazy. 'They want to know if I was ever arrested. I was arrested for littering, and therefore I can't go to Vietnam — great! They want me to go and kill people but they're not sure because I litter.' And that kind of tickled his fancy."

It would soon tickle many other people's fancies as well. It didn't matter whether or not it was really littering that kept Arlo out of the draft. The story of the little guy who escapes the clutches of a heartless bureaucracy because of its own pettiness and illogic proved to have a universal and timeless appeal, in spite of its 1960s setting. It became so ubiquitous at Thanksgiving that on that holiday in 1996, mission control in Houston woke up the astronauts on board the space shuttle *Columbia* with a recording of "Alice's Restaurant."

"Good morning from Houston and Alice's Restaurant," said spacecraft communicator Dominic Gorie.

"Good morning, Houston," astronaut Tom Jones replied. "We have our turkey steaks thawing out right now."

Of course the song was particularly relevant in the 1960s, as it addressed an issue that was on everyone's mind — the draft — with a perspective that was refreshingly different from the more common "Eve of Destruction" brand of protest song. Although it is generally described as a Woody Guthrie–style "talking blues" song, "Alice's Restaurant" is hardly blue. With its catchy chorus about Alice and the restaurant, it asks its listeners to "end the war and stuff" essentially by laughing at society's foibles.

Although "the long song" was a big hit in coffeehouses, Arlo never expected to hear it on the radio. "I didn't expect anything to happen," he once said. "No one in his right mind ever thought it would have gotten played on the radio. It was almost written in stone that you couldn't play anything over two and a half minutes."

Then, late one night in February 1967, Ramblin' Jack Elliot took Arlo along on a visit to WBAI, a nonprofit FM radio station then located on East 39th Street in New York City, in an office just below the Vera Institute of Justice. WBAI was a loosely formatted station broadcasting news of the Vietnam War, countercultural programs, and underground rock and roll. It was the kind of station where a young folk musician could stop by, play music, and chat with Bob Fass, the host of "Radio Unnamable," dubbed by some "The Father of Free-form Radio."

"I first heard about Arlo from someone who said he'd been playing in Stockbridge," Bob Fass recalls. "I said, 'Just because he's Woody's son doesn't mean he's good.' But she said, 'He's really good. You have to hear him.' Then one night Jack Elliot came up. We'd known each other since before I was on the radio. I liked it a lot when musicians brought people they thought were worth hearing. And he brought little Arlo."

As Arlo remembers it, Jerry Jeff Walker was also there that evening. The group squeezed into the cramped little studio, and the musicians took turns playing songs live on the air.

"Jerry Jeff sang 'Mr. Bojangles,' which everybody loved," Arlo told reporter Russell Hall, "and Jack sang a long song which eventually was called '912 Greens,' about a trip he made to New Orleans. Not to be outdone, I said, 'Hey, I've got one that's longer than that.'"

Today, Bob Fass says, it is hard to imagine hearing the words "Alice's Restaurant" and not associating them with Arlo, Vietnam, and littering, but at the time, he thought Arlo was about to sing a restaurant commercial. He was pleasantly surprised. Whenever Arlo came to the chorus, everyone in the studio sang along.

"It sounded like a congregation at a reformed synagogue with everyone trying to sing along with the prayers that they didn't quite know," the announcer recalls. Fortunately, Bob recorded the song, and Arlo gave him permission to play it on the air in the future. "In some ways the version that ended up on the record was better, but I like my version better. I thought it was more laconic, funnier, more intimate. The enthusiasm was just great."

The radio station was swamped with calls from listeners who wanted to hear more. Since the listener-supported station was running a fund drive, Bob decided to hold the song for "ransom." During fund drives, Bob liked to play games with his listeners. He would play songs they didn't want to hear, like "God Bless America" and "The Ballad of the Green Berets," over and over until callers had pledged enough money to make him stop. Alternately, he would start up a fund for a really popular song. When $1,000 in pledges had been gathered, he'd play the record. The studio recording of "Alice's Restaurant" earned enough to get on the air several times.

"They raised a lot of money," Arlo says. "To the point where they were playing the song so much people had to send in money to get them to stop."

The song wasn't on an album yet, but that didn't stop other stations in the area from getting copies of the tape. Those in the know wore "Alice's Restaurant" buttons. At one point someone climbed up on the Brooklyn Bridge at night and hung a huge banner reading ALICE'S RESTAURANT across it.

"Arlo will be a big name in a few months," predicted the *Underground Digest*. "A name to rank up or down there in elusive neon vapors with Buckley, Ochs, and Blue and perhaps Donovan. Already the word is out among the 'in' music set that Arlo is singing/talking in a decidedly different way. He's already said it on tape in a 25-minute number called 'Alice's Restaurant,' which has been blowing minds in New York on various 'with it' stations."

The song got its next big push at the Newport Folk Festival in July of that year. Arlo was slated to play his song at a topical song workshop on Saturday afternoon. It was such a hit that he played it the next afternoon for an audience of 3,500. The listeners were so taken with the song that the festival producer, George Wein, decided to have Arlo close the festival with "Alice." Thirty of the festival's famous folkies joined Arlo onstage to sing the chorus in front of an audience of 9,500. The next day the *New York Times* ran an article with the headline "Arlo Guthrie Festival Hero with 'Alice's Restaurant.'" Music critic John S. Wilson called it "the most unlikely hit song since 'Yes, We Have No Bananas.'" "Alice's Restaurant," the album, recorded at a cost of only $3,500, was released two months later.

Interestingly, WBAI moved in 1969 into a former Protestant church on East 62nd Street. The former sanctuary of the brick church was used as a performance space until the station was forced to move again because of city tax laws. The church was torn down shortly after the station moved out. A condominium complex now stands in its place; in the lobby is a photograph of the church that once stood there.

Woody Guthrie lived long enough for Arlo to play his breakthrough song for him. Harold Leventhal, manager to both artists, was there and said he saw a smile flicker across Woody's face. But Woody did not live to witness the song's success. He died October 3, 1967, as Arlo's career was taking off. According to Arlo, it is a family joke that "Woody heard the song and died."

"No one cried for Woody," Arlo once told a reporter. "You don't cry for a man when he's lived a good life and found a release from pain. You're happy for him."

"Alice's Restaurant" was a nationwide sensation, earning Arlo the somewhat uncomfortable dual mantle "spokesman of his generation and son of a legend." The critics, like Arlo before the shrink in room 604, raved.

"Just as Woody Guthrie drew from his Dust Bowl roots to become the definitive folk poet of the Depression, his son Arlo has become a forceful musical spokesman for another generation," wrote a *Washington Post* reviewer. "He is among the finest of this country's young singers and writers. Indeed, he may already be the best of the lot."

The *Toronto Daily Star* wrote: "The next folk hero in America will be a skinny, homely, rustic hippy from Brooklyn who plays good guitar and sings through his nose. His name is Arlo Guthrie."

"Stunning . . . a comic fable of the triumph of individualism over society," said the *Los Angeles Times*.

"The richly ornamented irony of Guthrie's prose and his superb sense of timing turn 'Alice's Restaurant' into a winsome, memorable addition to the antiwar repertory," wrote *Time*.

"The son of the late (but already legendary) Woody Guthrie will soon be something of a legend himself if he can continue in the brilliant pattern he establishes for himself in 'Alice's Restaurant,'" *Hi/Fi Stereo Review* wrote. "His description of his confrontations with psychiatrists and with other inductees who have police records will remain in my memory as one of the deadliest pieces of satire I have ever heard . . . It is one of the funniest, truest, most pointedly intelligent appraisals of our society that has come from anyone, young or old, in a very long time."

Arlo heard many stories of people actually singing the chorus of "Alice's Restaurant" before the draft board. Years later Jeff Tamarkin, writing for *Discoveries* magazine, would recall, "A phrase was often invoked by guys who had managed to avoid the draft. The phrase was 'pulled an Arlo.' What that meant was that, like the narrator of the Alice tale, you'd somehow managed to convince the United States military — by any means possible — that you just weren't going to do them much good in the rice paddies of Vietnam, and therefore you'd both be better off not getting involved with one another."

The song was even popular in Vietnam itself. Soldiers sent Arlo photographs of their own homemade Alice's Restaurants — a tent or a tin can in the middle of the jungle with a sign that said ALICE'S RESTAURANT. "I think those guys really needed to laugh every once in a while," Arlo says.

In all, the LP stayed on the album charts for ninety-nine weeks, peaking at number seventeen. It went platinum and continues to be a perennial seller for Warner Brothers. It was especially popular with the folks in the Berkshires who heard familiar names and places in the eighteen-minute ramble. They knew Officer Obie; they knew Alice and had eaten at her restaurant; they knew about the church and the people who hung out there. They laughed with a firsthand knowledge of how a simple littering arrest could be transformed into the "biggest crime of the last half-century" in their sleepy Massachusetts town.

Other residents were not as pleased with the song's celebrity. They were sure it would bring hippies by the busload to the Berkshires. They put up billboards reading KEEP AMERICA BEAUTIFUL, GET A HAIRCUT. The *Berkshire Eagle* editorial pages were filled with an ongoing debate they dubbed "Stockbridge Hippies Pro and Con." The stream of letters were printed with an editorial cartoon featuring the Stockbridge road sign and another sign reading CHECK POINT ARLO that listed requirements ("properly shorn" and "approved by the conformity commission") to enter the city. The debate began with a letter to the editor from Margaret W. Gray of Glendale dated February 5, 1968.

> When I was a child living in Stockbridge, the town would occasionally be visited by carloads of gypsies. Since they were regarded as light-fingered and undesirable, they were promptly told to leave by the police. Yesterday in Stockbridge, I saw a group of four or five so-called "hippies." Dirty long-haired and repulsive, they were the vanguard, no doubt, of the hordes that will descend on us this summer if something is not done to prevent it — the result of unfavorable publicity we have received from a recent song hit. Why should we have to put up with these revolting creatures? At best, they are a public eyesore; at worst, a threat to the health and morals of our young people. There is no reason why they should not be made to feel unwelcome as the gypsies were in the

past. Garbage has, indeed, been dumped in our town. Let us prevent any recurrent incident.

In truth, the region was not overrun by hippies searching for the setting of the song. For the most part, people outside of the Berkshires didn't pay enough attention to the details of the song to wonder about "the town of Stockbridge, Massachusetts, where this takes place" or the real Alice or Obie. But that quickly changed when film director Arthur Penn decided to use the story as the basis for a major motion picture.

❦

"The real interesting movie would be the movie of them making a movie of us."

— Steve Elliot

Stockbridge, March 1968

Before Hollywood came to town, there had been two distinct cultural elements in the area surrounding the former Trinity Church. There was the Establishment — the World War II generation — and the anti-Establishment baby boom generation. Then another group rolled into town with a culture all its own. Filmmakers observed the people of the New England village as subjects for their film, and the locals looked back at them with an equal amount of curiosity.

In case just having a film crew around was not quite surreal enough, *Alice's Restaurant* would blur fact and fiction to an enormous degree. There would be no "name" actors. The film would rely solely on the star power of the amiable but shy Arlo Guthrie, who offstage often spoke in half sentences and preferred not to be the center of attention.

Most of the young people who hung out at the church would play themselves, as would many of the townspeople. The result was a movie with scenes in which the real-life Arlo talks to an actress playing the role of Alice Brock, while the real-life Alice looks on in the role of one of her own friends; where Officer Obie plays himself doing things that weren't quite what he'd done in real life.

This strange scenario brought together some people who were formerly at odds and tore apart others who had been friends. Chief Obanhein began to view the young people in a new light, and they, in turn, came to understand him a little better. They could pretty much all agree: It was the movie people who were crazy.

Arlo Guthrie in 1968.

CLEMENS KALISCHER

"Almost everyone in Stockbridge heard the song 'Alice's Restaurant,'" Arlo says. "Some of them liked it, some of them didn't, but everyone heard it. Arthur Penn was a director who lived in Stockbridge. Where everyone else in the country heard the record and thought, 'What a creative guy that Arlo Guthrie is,' Arthur Penn said, 'He's not creative, he's telling the truth. There really is an Officer Obie; there really is a blind judge.' Arthur Penn said, 'I know these people. This guy is not making this stuff up.' He didn't know if the draft was true or not because he had no way of knowing that, but he came to me with a proposal. They wanted to make a movie of 'Alice's Restaurant,' and they wanted to use as many of the real people as possible."

The story of Alice, the restaurant, the church, and Arlo was especially familiar to the director, who divided his time between theater and film, because in 1967 he became president of the Berkshire Theatre Festival, a celebrated summer theater in Stockbridge. Alice's father, Joseph Pelkey, was a member of the board of trustees. Arthur knew Alice, he knew Ray, and he knew the kids. One day a few of Arlo's friends brought a copy of the record over and insisted the director listen to it. He thought the song was "a terrific portrait of what was going on at the time."

As it happened, that same evening he attended a party, and some of the well-heeled guests insisted that he listen to a record. It was, of course, "Alice's Restaurant." He remembers thinking, "If this group of stiffs thinks this is a wonderful record and the kids think this is a wonderful record, why not make a movie out of it?"

Arthur Penn was born September 27, 1922, in Philadelphia, the younger son of a watch maker and a nurse. (His older brother, Irving, became a photographer for *Vogue*.) During World War II, he served in Germany and Italy. When the war ended, he took a downgrade from sergeant to private to join a military show company. Following his service, he attended Black Mountain College in North Carolina and the Universities of Perugina and Florence in Italy. He thought he might follow in his father's footsteps and studied horology, the science of measuring time, but his real interest was television and movies. He began his television career as a floor manager for NBC and was assistant director of the Dean Martin– nbzJerry Lewis show in Hollywood. He went on to direct episodes of *Playhouse 90* and *Philco Playhouse*. From there he moved to the stage, directing Broadway productions of *The Miracle Worker* and Lillian Hellman's *Toys in the Attic*.

Arthur lived in Stockbridge and divided his time between his home there and the studios of New York City. By the time he started work on *Alice*, he had cemented his reputation for directing, as *Cineaste* magazine put it, "coming-of-age stories in which anguished protagonists undergo crucial and frequently violent transformations." His controversial depiction of Bonnie and Clyde redefined gangster movies and pushed the envelope for realistic violence on screen. The film, which starred Warren Beatty, Faye Dunaway, Gene Hackman, and Estelle Parsons, was one of the most talked-about films of the decade. It was lauded even as it was reproached for its uncritical depiction of violent acts combined with farce.

Arthur Penn on the set of Alice's Restaurant. *In the background are the real Alice Brock, Arlo Guthrie, and Pat Quinn, who played Alice in the movie.*

"In the late 1960s, the film's sympathetic characters appealed to American youth who were part of the countercultural movement protesting the Vietnam War and the U.S. government's role," wrote film critic Tim Dirks. "The influence of the film extended to commercial merchandise in the form of hairstyles, authentic period music of the 30s, and gangster retroclothing (such as the maxiskirt). The film also permanently changed the form and substance of popular films — for better or worse."

By the end of 1967, *Bonnie and Clyde* had earned $2.5 million. It was rereleased in 1968 and earned another $16.5 million. It was then one of the top twenty grossing pictures of all time. More than that, it helped define what was being called "the New Cinema."

In a cover story entitled "The New Cinema: Violence . . . Sex . . . Art," *Time* magazine's Stefan Kanfer called *Bonnie and Clyde* a "watershed picture," and "the best movie of the year." Characteristics of the New Cinema, he wrote, were a disregard for the pieties of plot, chronology, and motivation; a detached observation of events without presenting any conclusions; a blurring of the lines between comedy and tragedy, heroes and villains; and unrestrained sexuality.

Film commentator Peter Biskind wrote in *Easy Riders, Raging Bulls: How the Sex-Drugs-and-Rock 'n' Roll Generation Saved Hollywood*:

> In 1967, two movies, *Bonnie and Clyde* and *The Graduate*, sent tremors through the industry. This was to be a directors' decade if ever there was one. Directors as a group enjoyed more power, prestige and wealth than they ever had before. The great directors of the studio era, like John Ford and Howard Hawks, regarded themselves as nothing more than hired help paid to manufacture entertainment, story-tellers who shunned self-conscious style lest it interfere with the business at hand. New Hollywood directors, on the other hand, were unembarrassed — in many cases rightly so — to assume the mantle of the artist, nor did they shrink from developing personal styles that distinguished their work from that of other directors.

With his newfound prominence, Arthur Penn could probably have followed up *Bonnie and Clyde* with any movie he wanted. He chose *Alice's Restaurant*. One reason was strictly practical. He was going to be in Stockbridge over the summer anyway directing the play "A Matter of Position," and staying at home while working on a movie would be a nice change of pace.

"For years I've been building a pond here in Stockbridge," he once said. "It's just finished at last — and full. It's been my chief occupation. Making films seemed like a sideline."

But he was also drawn to the story for a number of artistic and commercial reasons. First, he identified with Arlo Guthrie's relationship with his father. When Arthur was in his late teens, he, too, took care of a dying father.

"There was something quite personal about that," he said in a 1969 *New York Times* interview. "My identity with Arlo's life, the hospital, Woody's dying, the inability to really articulate the feelings they were engaged in, Woody, physically, and Arlo psychologically. That was very much like the last year of my father's life. All I remember were the long silences."

Even more importantly, he identified with the former Stockbridge School kids. His alma mater, Black Mountain College, had been an experimental, countercultural school. Founded in 1933 by educator and critic of higher education John Andrew Rice, Black Mountain focused on art and stressed the benefits of the learning experience over reliance on grades.

"From this special community came a surprising number of the greatest artists of our time, a counterculture all its own," wrote Mary Holder, founder of the Black Mountain College Museum. "The atmosphere was often intense — freedom to learn, to create, to interrelate, to express — a sort of meeting place for artistic natures who were open and eager to learn through experimentation. And the unexpected. Basically, anything went."

Instructors at the college included Josef and Anni Albers, refugees from the Bauhaus, who taught art and weaving. Willem de Kooning, Buckminster Fuller, John Cage, and Merce Cunningham also briefly taught there. Fewer than twelve hundred students attended the school in its twenty-four years of operation, but among them were a number of prominent artists, including Robert Rauschenberg, Kenneth Noland, John Chamberlain, Kenneth Snelson, Dorothea Rockburne, Ray Johnson, Jose Yglesias, and Edward Dorn.

"It [the college] endured only fifteen years," Arthur told *Cineaste*. "We lived in a small community in North Carolina, we cooked our own food, grew a good portion of it, and a lot of wonderful people dropped in . . . It was a very attractive place, but at the same time it had the seeds of its own destruction within it. It couldn't last because it was a dream as much as *Alice's Restaurant* was a dream."

From what he knew of the church folks, they would be the perfect illustration not only of the hippie subculture, which was becoming more and more interesting to the moviegoing public, but also of the dream of a different society that he recalled from his own school days. Its church setting would give the story added depth and poignancy. It was a metaphor for their spiritual world, of new sets of beliefs replacing the old, perhaps of the void that is left when old structures are abandoned.

"It was important to have a pretty clear rendering of what was taking place with the youth in that period of what people called the counterculture — what I call the 'real culture,'" Arthur says. "They were really the true voice of the country at that time. It was about the community coming together, being important to people at a certain stage in their life and then as they get a little older and things change, as certain real events come into the community — death, loss, love. All of those come in, and then lo and behold, the community changes or, in this case, virtually ceases to exist. Sooner or later communities change greatly. I was very interested in the idea that a church had been desanctified, which was not in Arlo's record."

So it was probably not a straightforward love of the song that inspired Arthur Penn to make the film. Describing his plans to the Stockbridge selectmen, he called the song "simpleminded" and said that while the movie "would contain some elements of Arlo Guthrie's record, it would not be limited to it."

The song "Alice's Restaurant" had not been popular with everyone in Stockbridge. After all, it had hardly been a ringing endorsement of the Stockbridge establishment, especially the town's police. Selectmen were concerned that a cinematic version of the song might put the town in a bad light.

Penn assured them that his goal was to tell a more balanced story than the song had. He wanted to give Stockbridge residents "an opportunity to speak back, to offer comments, in a certain sense to offer another point of view . . . The way others involved remember the incident would be important to the picture . . . We have no intention of making fun of the town. But it is difficult to know what will offend people these days. It wouldn't be candid of me not to say the record makes a bit of a farce of the police department. The movie would probably do a little of that but would also set the record straight. I don't want to suggest there's any way I can assure everyone in town in advance whether or not they will be offended."

He added that *Alice's Restaurant* would be "a very light film," and that he hoped Officer Obanhein would play himself. The room broke into laughter when the police officer shook his head and said, "I should have picked up the rubbish myself."

In the winter of 1968 Arthur Penn invited a bunch of the kids who'd spent time at the church to his house to discuss making the movie. As the director recalled in an introduction to the screenplay, "We smoked some, and when we talked about the draft they unleashed a flood of

Screenwriter Venable Herndon goes over the script with Arlo.

tales about their physical and psychological experiences at their draft examinations . . . We smoked some more, then Arlo played 'Amazing Grace' for about two hours and we hummed, sang, wailed or went along. Then they left."

Arthur Penn asked screenwriter Venable Herndon to come on board and help convert the song into a movie. Venable, who today is a screenwriting professor at NYU, was described by Alice as "a fascinating guy with an incredible mind." He grew up in a working-class household and attended Princeton and Harvard. He had just completed the screenplay for an Otto Preminger film called *Too Far to Walk,* which was never produced.

Arthur and Venable agreed that the deconsecrated church would serve not only as the setting but also as the central motif of the film. So they began by discussing the project with Reverend Whitman at the diocese and Reverend Middleton at St. James Church.

Venable remembers the single sentence that gave him the idea for the structure of the script. While he was interviewing Reverend Whitman about the history of the building, the minister said, "I deconsecrated that fabric."

"It never occurred to me you had to deconsecrate a church," Venable says. "I was raised Episcopalian, but by a father who mostly sat in the car reading the *New York Times* while he sent me in with the money for the collection. So I got to thinking, if society has deconsecrated the church, can an alternative community reconsecrate the church? The answer was no. At least I think that was the answer."

Arthur Penn, meanwhile, asked Reverend Middleton if he knew what words had been used at the deconsecration ceremony. The minister knew the words exactly, because they were in *The Book of Offices.* Arthur asked him if he would be willing to don his robe and perform the ceremony for the film. Reverend Middleton said he would.

"It was my first speaking part in a film," he says with a laugh.

Reverend Whitman, who actually performed the ceremony, says that he was disappointed that he was not asked to reprise his real-life role. "In the movie I'm not the one who does it," he says good-naturedly. "I was a little annoyed with a friend of mine, Reverend Middleton, because he took my part. I think he wanted to do it. No one asked me."

For about six months before shooting on the movie began, Venable stayed in a motel in Great Barrington. When he was not writing or meeting with the director, he was interviewing the principal characters in the story and hanging out at the church, observing everyday life.

"I was kind of suspended between two worlds," Venable remembers. "There was the world of Arthur Penn and the world of the church. I somehow, without getting involved emotionally or sexually, managed to just hang around. They didn't stop doing anything because I was there. They sort of ignored me in the good sense that I was able to be part of their lives and get to know them. There were various young kids living in the church, but they actually weren't doing much. Everything that went on was the daily-ness, the unstructured daily-ness of their lives."

Venable saw in the young people a modern version of Brook Farm, an 1840s experiment in communal living in West Roxbury, Massachusetts. The farm, which lasted from 1841 to 1847, was established by Unitarians, although most of the members had left that church and were advocates of transcendentalism. The group included many prominent artists and intellectuals: Nathaniel Hawthorne, John S. Dwight, Charles A. Dana, and Isaac Hecker. People like Ralph Waldo Emerson, W. E. Channing, Margaret Fuller, Horace Greeley, and Orestes Brownson also spent time there. The Brocks' church, in Venable's mind, "was more a sanctuary in the medieval sense than the earlier, more enlightened, transcendental experiment."

"The whole Vietnam thing had really taken over in terms of feeling," he recalls. "There was a great deal of pain about the whole thing. It's hard to imagine now how many people were going off in the country in Massachusetts, and Vermont and New Hampshire, and just sort of living on farms. It sounds very odd today, but in those days it was almost routine. The church and the group were emblematic of a movement, but they were far from unique. Such a film could have been written about people who lived on a farm, but the emblem of the church was different because it was so specific. Here, where we had celebrated one kind of ritual, we're now doing something else. It's not like we went from milk cows to hippies. Now here were the hippies in the church."

The screenwriter was interested in everyday life at the church and did not delve too deeply into people's backgrounds. He assumed the kids came from working-class homes. Since private boarding schools were hardly a sign of status in the hippie subculture, this aspect of their story was not discussed much. Even if it had been, it would probably have been downplayed in the film. The only reference to how the kids met Alice and Ray in the picture was one line spoken by Arlo. "I remember when you used to run the library at school," he tells Alice. "We used to check out books just to see you."

The film also makes no reference to Ray's career, because Venable never knew what Ray's career was. "When I met him, it seemed like he was in a time in his life when he wasn't really doing anything for a living."

The original vision was to depict a truly multiracial hippie community. Rick Robbins, "the other litterbug," was transformed into "Arlo's Negro friend Roger" in the original screenplay. Arlo's girlfriend in the movie was to be "a tall Japanese-Spanish girl." If Venable Herndon had had his way, he says, the script might have been more political than it was.

"I wrote some stuff which Arthur didn't want," he says. "I was, in a sense, a little more radical than he was. He had to make sure it would work for a general audience."

One line that was cut involved the character Jake, a friend who had lost his hand in the war. At one point the characters are carrying furniture into a building and someone says, "Can someone give us a hand?" Jake raises his hook and replies, "I already did."

"This was kind of a crude joke, I guess," Venable says. "It was my bitterness against the Vietnam War, and that's the kind of joke he took out, and probably rightly so."

None of the people who were depicted in the film were involved in the writing of the script. As Venable recalls, everyone was cooperative and excited about being in a movie, "although they didn't express that to me. That would be kind of embarrassing to say, 'I'm excited about being in a movie.' They wanted to play it cool. I don't know if [the Brocks] were happy to be, in a sense, celebrated. I always found Alice to be a lovely, cooperative, interesting woman. I don't remember anyone objecting or trying to interfere in any way with the making of the film."

Arlo says he was never asked to be involved in the writing, nor did it cross his mind to ask to be involved. "I was still basically nineteen or something. I had no skills as a writer anyway, let alone as an actor. The movie wanted to talk about the troubles of youth in America, communes in America, the search for a new way of life, none of which interested any of us. We saw it as an opportunity to be in a movie."

Alice and Ray Brock on the set of Alice's Restaurant.

Once they had their subject, the next step for the filmmakers was to secure the rights to use real people's identities in the movie. They got permission from Chief Obanhein and Judge Hannon as well as Ray and Alice Brock.

Arlo's 18-^{1}/$_2$-minute story-song took up only a few pages of the completed script. Arlo would not even be the central character. The main characters in the drama would be Ray and Alice Brock and an entirely fictional character, a heroin addict named Shelly.

"We put that in to give it a kind of structure," Venable explains. "Because his ups and downs are part of a dramatic structure. You have to have the audience identify with the protagonist. Then you throw the obstacles against the protagonist, and the obstacles are either overcome or the obstacles overcome the protagonist. That's basic film structure. In fact, Arlo didn't have to go through anything like that. He is more or less a commenting, singing, comic figure."

Of the real-life characters, the focus would especially be on Alice, whose name was in the title. As Robin Wood wrote: "'Remember Alice?' Arlo asks about a third of the way through the record. In the film we are in no danger of forgetting her."

When Alice signed her contract with the moviemakers, she had split from Ray and was living in Boston, so she was one of the last to be contacted about the project. Venable says he would have liked to see Alice in the role of Alice but that Arthur Penn was "a little bit frightened by the proposition." For his part, Arthur says he simply wanted a professional actress in what was arguably the most demanding role in the film. In the end Alice was not asked to play herself, and she says she would not have wanted to.

"My father and Arthur Penn had worked together in the Berkshire Theatre Festival," she says. "My father called me up in Boston. He said, 'Arthur Penn is thinking of doing this, and I want you to cooperate totally with him--and he's going to pay you.' I didn't really like the idea, but my father was a real bully, and he had promised he would deliver me. I got a little more money than Arthur Penn offered me. It didn't occur to anyone that it was going to have any effect on your life. We never saw anything like that. We never saw people like that. We never saw that kind of money being spent. We'd never seen a movie being shot. The whole thing was a brand-new experience for us. We thought we were getting paid a fortune. He paid the people a hundred dollars a week. That was unbelievable money for doing nothing. I remember reading that contract. I was signing away the rights to my life and everything about it, and anything they may ever want to make up about it, and these rights would go on forever, and his children's children would have those rights to my story and anything they wanted to add or subtract from my story. They said, that's the standard contract. That's not a standard contract! Movies weren't made like that often — about people who are still alive who weren't public figures to begin with. It's not like I was Dwight Eisenhower or Audie Murphy. We were just human beings. If he could have, he would have paid me two thousand dollars for the whole thing, but I got a lawyer. So what did I get, about eight thousand dollars for the whole thing." (Ray received $1,000 for the rights to his story, plus $500 a week for renting out the church.)

In September John J. Dwyer and Judge James Hannon held a party and announced that Arthur Penn had received permission to film in the county and that shooting was set to begin October 1, to take advantage of the beautiful fall foliage in the Berkshires. The two judges said they had read the script and "found nothing derogatory in any way" toward the towns involved or the county. Filming would take place in many parts of the county, including the Lee District Court, the Lee police lockup, the small restaurant in Stockbridge formerly owned by Alice Brock, and the former Trinity Church in Van Deusenville.

Where's Arlo? The sanctuary filled to capacity with extras for the wedding scene in Alice's Restaurant.

"Shine light on electrons
You'll cause them to swerve
The act of observing
Disturbs the observed."
— L. M. Boyd

Stockbridge, October 1968

W ith a go-ahead from United
Artists, a completed screenplay, and permission to film in the Berkshires,
all that remained was to assemble a cast. Even before the script had been
finished, Arthur Penn had been asking local residents to reprise their
real-life roles. Most of the "Establishment" figures in Arlo's story quickly
agreed to take part.

If "everyone wanted to be in the newspaper story" about the littering arrest, it seemed that everybody and his brother wanted to be in the
movie about it. More than two decades later Arlo would tell a *Berkshire
Eagle* reporter about his amusement when the soldiers at the induction
center on Whitehall Street in New York City asked if they could have
cameos: "All these guys who gave me a hard time were saying, 'Excuse
me, Mr. Guthrie, can I be in the movie?' and I'd say, 'Sure, stand over
there.'"

Arthur Penn (left) and Bill Obanhein (center) review the script for Alice's Restaurant *with first assistant director William Geritty Jr.*

Bill Obanhein, though initially relunctant to participate, became the low-key scene-stealer of the film. In the end he lost thirty pounds during the shoot and gained the nickname "One-shot Obie."

"He was the easiest on the film to work with," Arlo says. "With me it was always take sixty-four, but with him, the first time he shot it, that was it."

Arthur Penn called him "just about the best nonprofessional actor I ever worked with." His sympathetic on-screen presence probably improved upon the public image the song had created of this representative of the Establishment. Working so closely with the young people definitely improved his image of them. "My life is the same, but my attitudes have changed," he told a reporter. "I realize that kids with long hair and weird-looking clothes can be basically nice people."

Alice told a reporter that working with the officer had been a step forward in hippie/police relations. "Bill Obanhein was sincere, he was trying, and he didn't like it at all," she said. "I'll bet the movie changed Obie's life more than it changed anyone else's because a lot of people in the town thought the chief of police shouldn't be involved in such a thing. I fell in love with him. I found out he was a human being. He's a really beautiful guy."

The film would also give temporary employment to many young people. Almost everyone Arlo knew — and some "friends" he didn't — was in the movie somewhere.

The twelve-week production employed one thousand locals as actors and about thirty more as electricians, carpenters, and handymen. More than $1 million in salaries alone was pumped into the Berkshires economy.

The majority of the extras were excited at the idea of being in a movie — and of being paid. Extras received $75 to $100 a week, which was a substantial sum in 1968. They were also excited about the subject matter. If their experience could be translated into a film that could capture the feeling they shared, it would have to be a pretty good movie. A few, however, were somewhat reluctant to let the public into their lives.

"Arlo wanted his friends to work on it and make some money," Paul Kleinwald says. "I was making seventy-five dollars a week, or a hundred — whatever I was making at the time, they paid me twice that. So I was all for it. I signed up right away."

Rick Robbins says he decided against playing Arlo's littering friend in the movie. The role went instead to Geoff Outlaw, Arlo's friend from grade school.

"For the past thirty years I've been able to place the blame on Geoff Outlaw because he's the one who played me in the movie," Rick says. "People would say, 'Are you the guy who was arrested with Arlo?' And I'd say, 'Me? No, go see the movie — that guy didn't look anything like me.' I didn't play myself in the movie because it rubbed me the wrong way. I'm not saying Arlo did something wrong. Arlo did a great thing for his career, but I rebelled against it. I was in it in a couple of shots, but I am embarrassed by the movie. The dialogue was so far away from the way we felt."

As Geoff remembers it, both he and Rick wanted to play the part. He says they tossed a coin to see who would have the role, and he won.

"The idea that there were vast numbers of hippies living in this church as a commune is totally false," Arlo says. "It was never a commune. There were never large herds of anybody. But when we were making this movie, it was an excuse to get all these people together because they were getting paid twenty dollars a day. And all these out-of-work hippies were saying, 'Yeah, yeah, I'm friends with Arlo,' and all my friends I went to school with, all the people that Ray and Alice knew, were extras in the movie, so everyone in the movie is basically a friend with somebody. That was the wide circle of acquaintances. We all knew somebody who knew somebody who knew somebody. That's who was in the movie, all of our girlfriends, boyfriends . . ."

The cast was rounded out with professional actors in key roles, although even the professionals had limited cinematic experience. James "Jimmy" Broderick, who played Ray Brock, was the closest thing to a screen veteran. He grew up in New Hampshire and went to New York in the 1940s to become an actor. He had appeared in one film and a variety of television series, including *As the World Turns* in the role of Jim Norman. He would go on to be best known for his role in the 1976 televison series *Family*. In 1968, however, he was hardly a household name.

"My dad did a few musicals and was very unlucky," his son, Matthew Broderick, once said. "On Broadway, he had a show close in one night. He had a beautiful [singing] voice that people rarely heard."

Articles about Arlo Guthrie rarely fail to mention that he is the son of "legendary folksinger" Woody Guthrie. Similarly, Jimmy Broderick often appears in articles about his son, fellow actor Matthew. Matthew was the youngest of three children born to Jimmy and his wife, Patricia, a playwright and director. Jimmy was Episcopalian; his wife was Jewish. Although Matthew considers himself "more Jewish than anything else," one of his two older sisters is an ordained Episcopalian priest. Matthew loved to hang out backstage during his father's theatrical performances, but he never planned to become an actor himself. He

CLEMENS KALISCHER

James Broderick as Ray Brock.

discovered, however, that acting came quite naturally. His first professional role, at eighteen, was opposite his father in Horton Foote's play
On Valentine's Day. Two years later he was set to appear in *Torch Song
Trilogy*, a role that would launch his career. The night of the first preview
of the play, James Broderick learned he had cancer. He died on the night
of the first rehearsal for *Brighton Beach Memoirs*, for which Matthew would
win a Tony Award.

"My wanting to be an actor was very tied into my father being one,
so it was very strange for all of this to be going on while he was dying,"
Matthew Broderick told a *Newsday* reporter. "He was just a great spirit,

The two Alices: Alice Brock and actress Pat Quinn.

a wonderful man. He wasn't particularly narcissistic, but he loved his work, and was really strict about being responsible and professional about it. He tried to pass that on to me."

Jimmy Broderick was always well-groomed and dressed conservatively in outfits by Paul Stuart and Brooks Brothers. In Alice's mind, he was far from the obvious choice to portray Ray Brock, who normally dressed in jeans and had unruly hair and a disheveled, mutinous look about him.

"The guy they picked to play Ray was a really sweet man," Alice says. "A really nice man and an excellent actor, but totally miscast. And the part was totally miswritten. Arthur Penn would rather meet four thousand cannibals at midnight than have to deal with Ray Brock. Ray was just too big a presence, too big and scary."

Geoff, on the other hand, felt that the actor's portrayal was too crazy. "Ray was not the maniac that Jimmy played him as in the movie. The real Ray was more elegant than Jimmy Broderick was. Ray was a southern gentleman. He was an Old World southern gentleman."

Pat Quinn, who would portray Alice, had appeared off-Broadway and in a few small roles in television series like *Gunsmoke, Dr. Kildare,* and *Judd for the Defense.* She came to the production straight from a California stock theater company. Michael McClanathan, as the drug-addicted Shelly, and Tina Chen, as Arlo's girlfriend, Mari-Chan, had never been in a movie before, although Tina had appeared in a television special, for which she received an Emmy nomination. They were all thrust into an unusual acting situation. They would play their roles while being observed by members of the very community they were pretending to be part of — in Pat Quinn's and James Broderick's case, by the very people they were pretending to be.

"Pat Quinn, who played me, was told not to spend any time with me and not to be influenced by me at all," Alice says. "She picked up a few mannerisms, but they knew how they wanted her to be and they didn't want her to be influenced by me."

Tina Chen's character (the "Japanese-Spanish girl"), on the other hand, was not based on anyone in particular. "My character could have been anybody," she says. "It just sort of happened that it was an Asian-American that played that part. I remember having a very good time, because it was my first film. I was a little more naive than the rest of the cast members. I was brought up a little stricter than a lot of the members. Some of them are older. I played a character that related to that sixties time. Everyone was freer and experimenting and fun, and I kept to myself and read lots of books. It was in that era that I knew lots of things were going on. Lots of free sex. I'm not saying that anybody had it; but if someone was good-looking, then there would be a lot of females surrounding the person. I was more of an observer than a participant. If there were any problems or if anyone was on something, I didn't know about it."

Filming began with scenic outdoor shots, then moved to the church in Van Deusenville. The century-old building would not take the rigors of being a film set without a little help. The crew first went into the church

CLEMENS KALISCHER

Tina Chen reads a book on the set of Alice's Restaurant. Behind her are Paul Kleinwald (with guitar) and Sprage Baldwin.

basement and reinforced the floor to take the weight of all the people and machinery. In the scene in which motorcycles speed through the church door, it might have appeared as if a board was merely balanced on the steps, but a great deal of construction was required to meet safety standards.

Next, they rigged lights and camera platforms in the rafters with ropes. Extra power lines were added to bring more electricity into the building. The lights, cameras, and other equipment were brought to the church in six large vans. Everything smelled of plywood, the basic material of movie sets. The lights and the crowds in the sanctuary heated it and created a summerlike temperature inside, although it was unseasonably cool outside.

Because the early scenes in the film were to show the young people moving in and doing repairs on the church, set artists tore down some of what had been built so they could show the building in progress in the movie. They put in hours of work performing such tasks as painting cracks on the walls by hand to give the building a run-down look. The stained-glass windows that had been broken in 1962, precipitating the sale of the church to the Brocks, were fixed after a fashion. The set crew made colorful laminates that they used to cover the plain glass of any imperfect windows.

Across the street from the church was a mobile Kentucky Fried Chicken stand to feed the crew and extras. Cast members napped on cots and in the vestibule of the church. There were cars parked everywhere. Extra police were on duty to keep the peace.

The film crew also had to deal with Ray Brock, who was not always pleased with what they were doing to his home. On one memorable occasion, Ray arrived just as the set designers were cutting a limb off one of his trees. Ray was incredulous that they would take such liberties for the sake of one shot. After some shouting and waving of arms he calmed down, and filming resumed.

The snow came early that year, forcing the crew to film a number of scenes in early November around heavy, blowing snow. Arthur Penn had come down with a virus just as work on the film began. He was feeling ill and taking medication throughout much of the shoot.

Arthur's directorial style, while wonderful for the actors in a particular scene, baffles anyone else who tries to make sense of the production. He takes very few notes and makes few lists. He never shares what he says to one actor with another actor. The result is that most of the people on the set, even those playing in a given scene, have little idea how the finished product will look. During filming, the only one with a complete vision of *Alice's Restaurant* was Arthur Penn.

Venable Herndon says, "If you've ever been on a film set, it begins as a great muddle in the morning, and all day long there's this table of food set out. The only people who know what's going on are the cameramen, the lighting directors, and the director. If you're hanging around, as I was hanging around, even as the writer of the thing, you're not looking through the camera. You don't know what's going to show up at the end of the day in terms of what's going to be cut together."

According to the local paper, neighbors were complaining that the film about littering was creating too much litter. "The selectmen reported last night that they had received several complaints from residents in the Van Deusenville section of Housatonic that the movie crew has left excessive litter. The crew has been filming at the well-known Van Deusenville 'hippie church' for the past several weeks . . . The board agreed to write officials of the film company asking their cooperation in reducing the alleged litter in the area."

"It was chaos," Rick Robbins recalls. "People were trying to get a little piece of the action, get their pictures taken, see the stars. And other celebrities showed up — Claire Bloom. It was a Hollywood scene. It was absurd. We had this view of the church as our little sanctuary away from everybody and all of a sudden we were in the spotlight. It was horrible."

Alice was not impressed with the Hollywood crowd either. "They were in a business where you're trying to get stuff from people without letting them know how much you're getting from them. We had nothing to do with those kind of people, but all of a sudden there they were in our faces. We blew their minds more than they blew our minds. A lot of the people involved in the movies left the business, moved to the Berkshires, let their hair grow long."

Most of the film's key sequences took place in the church. The deconsecration scene was probably the most historically accurate, except for the row of stage lights mounted to the ceiling that are clearly visible in long shots of the sanctuary. Thanksgiving and the litter dumping events were recreated, not the way they actually happened but in the exaggerated and humorous way they were described in Arlo's song. After Thanksgiving dinner, the many visitors load up the red VW microbus with, literally, "shovels and rakes and implements of destruction" — well, a push mower, anyway. Officer Obie, as himself, with what film critic Robert Hatch called "a tone of baffled outrage tempered by curiosity," arrests and handcuffs Arlo and his fictional friend Roger, played by his real friend Geoff, puts them in the real cell, and takes out the toilet seat so they can't hit themselves over the head and drown.

Obie would later insist to a *Playboy* reporter, "I didn't take the toilet seats off, 'cause we don't have any seats. I told the architect who designed the cells you can't have things like that 'cause when people come in here, they're likely to rip them off."

The action then moved to the Lee Courthouse. The film circus drew a crowd wherever it went. "Main Street girl watchers" were especially interested in "a shapely young lady sporting bell-bottom trousers, dark felt hat, and hair down over her shoulders. She was said to be the leading lady," the *Berkshire Eagle* reported.

The brief scene at the courthouse shows the young litterers brought to trial before Judge Hannon and his Seeing Eye dog, Susie, both playing themselves. Obie, sitting over his five or six eight-by-ten black and white photos, begins to cry. The boys then pick up the garbage and drive off "into the sunset." Well, sort of . . .

The sunset was filmed at Tom Hebner's farm. One day Tommy came home with the famous movie director in tow. Arthur Penn wanted permission to do one scene on the hill behind the Hebners' house. They were thrilled to be part of the production. After drafting a contract to absolve the Hebners of liability for any injuries or mishaps on the hill, the film crew spent two afternoons trying to capture a sunset. But the sun refused to cooperate. It sank too fast, it was too low, and it didn't silhouette. The crew finally set up the cameras facing uphill so that as the actors headed up toward the midafternoon sun, they looked as if they were riding off into the sunset.

Adding to the surreal quality of the project was Arlo's acting performance. A natural on the stage, he seemed to be uncomfortable in the role of Arlo Guthrie on film. Arlo himself often jokes, "I only made one movie . . . because I saw it."

"Sometimes it's very hard to locate Arlo's performance," editor Dede Allen told *Show* magazine. "He can't really control himself consciously in a performance. He doesn't really know what he's giving off. Sometimes Arthur needs five or six takes to get even a little of that unusual quality Arlo has."

It's possible that Arlo was simply acting a little too well. In groups he often stands to one side, his body still but his eyes engaged, watching the people around him with clear interest. When Arthur Penn asked Arlo to do what he would really be doing in a scene, Arlo would give him exactly that.

His acting was adept enough to land him another acting role, albeit not for another thirty years. In 1994 he was asked to audition for an ABC drama produced by Stephen Bochco, the man behind *NYPD Blue*, who was reportedly impressed with his work in *Alice's Restaurant*. Arlo auditioned for the role of an aging hippie who returns to high school in the series *Byrds of Paradise*. His acting had apparently improved over the years, or perhaps he was just more comfortable playing a character who was not named "Arlo." He read a scene in which the character interviews for the job of housekeeper.

"So listen, man, I just hope I get the gig," he said.

Bochco leaned over and told him, "You just did."

The climax of *Alice's Restaurant* is a huge party at the church. More than two hundred people appear in the scene, which depicts a real-life event, a renewal wedding that Alice and Ray held after one of their separations in 1967. The walls of the church are decorated with paper flowers and shapes. A long banquet table is laden with food of all kinds. There are balloons everywhere, and all the extras are wearing elaborate costumes and face paint. Arlo's costume is supposed to be the king of cups from a deck of tarot cards.

"The movie was costumed much more elegantly than we ever were," Arlo says. "We all wore just blue jeans and T-shirts and stuff."

Tina Chen provided her own costume for the scene, a Chinese outfit that had belonged to her grandmother. After they finished the scene, the film company put it in storage. "They took it away from me because they said they wanted to make sure everything is OK, in case anything had to be refilmed and they would need it. As a youngster you don't think. So instead of me saying, 'No, you're not going to do that — this is my grandmother's,' I said OK. Everybody wrapped and left, and I tried to trace it much later. I never got it back."

The real Alice and Ray, recently divorced, were among the guests at the fictional Brocks' wedding. Pat Quinn, coincidentally, had just married a Cuban-born actor named Octavio Garcia. According to *Newsweek*, as the actress walked to the altar for the movie wedding ceremony, she passed the real Alice sitting by the aisle and whispered, "Better luck next time." The magazine quoted Alice as saying it was "a psychodrama a millionaire couldn't afford."

Saul Braun was on the set that day, reporting for *Playboy*: "Pat Quinn

CLEMENS KALISCHER

Tina Chen in her long-lost costume and Arlo Guthrie as a tarot card.

kisses Jimmy Broderick. That is, 'Alice' kisses 'Ray' and remarkably, this woman standing on the sidelines pales, her cheeks sinking and hardening. I go over to her and Benno introduces me and, of course, it is Alice herself."

The last moment of the wedding scene — of the entire film — was to be an image of Alice alone on the church steps contemplating the party that had somehow ended on a melancholy note. According to Venable Herndon, Arlo had a different idea for the end of film. "Arlo, I think, had expected the last shot to be of him playing the guitar and singing. But he didn't have any authority over the cutting."

Arthur Penn's concept was to symbolize Alice's feelings about the loss of her paradise by creating the illusion of freezing time, using a special camera shot that had been planned months before shooting began. He would dolly back a great distance, and yet it would not appear to the audience that they were moving away, because the camera zoomed in at the same time. The crew discovered, however, that if they didn't pass any objects, the viewer did not get the sense of tracking back. So they cut some trees and slid the stumps into the frame in just the right places; as they pulled back, the stumps were revealed, but the image of Alice did not get smaller. After lingering on that image, the scene faded to black.

"I wanted a certain melancholy in that scene," Arthur told the *New York Times*. "It was the closure of a phase in someone's life. I wanted the constancy of a memory experience and the physical sense of departure."

Arthur worked for hours on the film's final moments with editor Dede Allen. "I get uncomfortable looking at it that long," she said of the shot.

"That's exactly what I want," he replied.

The scene created the effect the director had wanted. It is a wistful, chilling moment. The last scene of the film left movie viewers with two images, the church and Alice. From that moment on, both would be famous.

"People come up and ask me for my autograph. I find it hard to say no to them because it makes them so happy. They're thrilled to meet Alice of 'Alice's Restaurant.' I'm a symbol of something that was meaningful to them."

— Alice Brock

New York, 1969

A *lice's Restaurant*, the movie, opened August 24, 1969, one week after the Woodstock Festival. The aptly named "exploitation materials" that United Artists sent to theater owners proclaimed that the sixty-second preview of the R-rated feature had "a lot going for it in selling *Alice's Restaurant*. The music, the famous recording, the great story, the hippies, the motorcyles and the whole exciting psychedelic bit!" The studio printed banners, flags, and badges with the slogan ALICE'S RESTAURANT: WHERE THE HEADS OF ALL NATIONS MEET, and suggested a number of promotional tie-ins, including unofficially naming a local restaurant "Alice's" for the duration of the showing.

Filmed for $2 million, *Alice's Restaurant* recouped that amount in three months. It went on to earn $6.3 million at the box office and an Oscar nomination for best director. (John Schlesinger won the Oscar for

Midnight Cowboy.) Arlo's compositions were nominated for the Anthony Asquith Award for Film Music at the British Academy Awards. (Burt Bacharach took that award for the music to *Butch Cassidy and the Sundance Kid*.) *Newsweek*, the *New York Times*, and *Life* all gave the film positive reviews. *Time* called it "one of the best films about young people ever made." Arthur Penn said he was surprised by the film's success, "as any sane person would be."

The album "Alice's Restaurant" had already sold 200,000 copies before the film was released. After its release another 100,000 were sold. There was also a soundtrack album, released on the United Artists label. "United Artists Records has issued a long-playing album of the film's original music, and it's the kind that's currently rocking the country," the promotional materials raved. "Any number of variations on displays in windows and counters of record shops suggest themselves. Remember the elements: the UA album, Arlo, the new popular folk singer and son of the famous 'Woody,' and of course the record itself." The soundtrack recording reached number sixty-three on the album charts.

Arlo appeared on the covers of *Newsweek* and *Esquire*. But there was more than enough fame to go around. *Look* and *Life* did photo spreads on the "church people," and *Playboy* ran an article on Alice and Ray. Bill Obanhein and Alice were both included in the 1970 edition of *Who's Who*. When Officer Obanhein was on the job, directing traffic, kids would shout out their car windows, "Hey, Obie!"

"Now all of a sudden it was like 'Oh, Alice.' All of a sudden I was becoming famous," Alice says. "People, even friends, didn't treat me the same because I was a star and I had my picture in the newspaper and magazines. Life was never the same."

Alice did not have an unlisted telephone number, and she frequently received calls from well-intentioned people from as far away as California. Sometimes, touched by the movie, they would call in the middle of the night to say they felt sorry for her.

The church, too, became famous — or infamous, depending on your point of view. People made their way to the Berkshires to see the landmark, to stand in front of it and have their pictures taken. Some even knocked on the door and asked for a tour.

In 1970, *Washington Post* reporter Ellen Hoffman described her own trek in search of the church.

Alice's church still stands in the same place near Van Deusenville — "It's all painted now so you can hardly recognize it"' one native warned. We attempted to find the church before getting on the road home from Stockbridge on Sunday morning, and every white barn and house seemed to take on the appearance of a church at a slight distance. We drove up to one abandoned house of worship next door to the Glen Dale, Mass., post office and tentatively peered in the window, even though we knew the location was wrong. When the postmistress came out of her house to watch us, we asked her if the church were Alice's. She said no and muttered something about "that damn thing" in a tone that seemed to indicate we were not the first ones to be mistaken.

The parade of tourists slowed over the years but never stopped, and their sense of direction has not improved much. As recently as 1998, a couple of midwestern teenagers made headlines when they cut school and headed to Massachusetts in search of the famous hippie church, which they thought was in Stockbridge. They didn't check their maps too carefully, though, and ended up in Worcester.

The "Stockbridge Hippies Pro and Con" debate was reopened on a national scale. After *Life* ran its feature, Margaret W. Gray sent a letter to the editor of the magazine repeating many of her complaints against the garbage-dumping hippies. But the Reverend Edwin Nettleton of St. John's Church in Center, Texas, had a different view of the community. "Looking at the picture of the 'church people' celebrating their Thanksgiving Eucharist I have the feeling that, though its name has been struck from the Episcopal Church Annual, here is a church that is alive and well and perhaps as consecrated as ever."

Nettleton was not in the majority among the Episcopal hierarchy, however. In the wake of the movie and the church's newfound fame as a countercultural landmark, the bishop of western Massachusetts ruled that in the future any church in the parish that had to be deconsecrated would be torn down rather than be allowed to be used in ways that would be, in the words of Reverend Middleton, "disturbing to the faithful."

Just five years later an international conference of representatives of religious institutions, businesses, and historic preservation and conservation groups was held in New York City to address what was becoming a growing problem throughout the world: what to do with "underused church property and the search for alternatives" as economic and cultural trends made it more difficult to sustain churches in the way they had been. The conference was held at Trinity Church in New York City, the most famous of architect Richard Upjohn's designs.

"The church represents the most compelling reason for preservation: a sense of history, a sense of eternity, a sense of greatness and a sense of community," said Beverly Moss Spatt, the chairperson of the Landmarks Commission of the City of New York. "If a modern society cannot understand religion as a pressing need, the church itself must bear the burden and attempt to preserve itself by making adjustments. We believe this adjustment is the key to preservation of churches — introduce new uses, recycle, add additional uses to complement the original function, restore their role as an important focus of the community."

Also at the conference was Giorgio Cavaglieri of the American Institute of Architects. "Even when a congregation is breaking away or diminishing in numbers, you should never consider destroying a church," he said. "The tearing down of a church should never exist . . . The church exists because it was built as a gathering point, as an auditorium, as a seating arrangement, a gathering point for people from the community that remains even when the congregation is gone. There are many other ways to gather with our fellow men. All those ways are suitable uses for a church building."

It is unclear whether the fame of *Alice's Restaurant* was instrumental in bringing this issue to the fore. In any case the movie had a dramatic impact on both the old Trinity Church and on the lives of those whose stories it told.

The movie is real life painted with the broad brush strokes of a screenplay. In her book *Rock Films*, Linda J. Sandahl wrote: "With a cast mainly of non-actors, Penn directs the story of the Alice's Restaurant Massacree almost like a home movie, and as such it can be very enjoyable." It seems so much like a home movie, in fact, that most viewers are convinced it is a documentary. Many are surprised to learn, for example, that Arlo's wife of thirty years is not Asian. Most of the people who have seen the film have never met Alice or Ray or even Arlo. What they know of them, they know from the movie. The fictionalized stories have taken on a life of their own; they are in some senses more real than reality.

By necessity, the real-life stories were altered in some places to heighten the drama and simplified in others. Arthur Penn says he never tried to tell the facts exactly as they were. He was just making a movie.

"I wasn't trying to be whatever 'real' is," he says. "I was trying to tell a story. A couple years ago Arlo said to me, 'We made the first music video.' And that's really what it is."

Even Venable Herndon says he does not know how much of the movie was real and how much was fiction. "I wish I could help you there," he says with a hearty laugh. "I don't know. To give you an example: In *Little Big Man* [Arthur Penn's next film], in the book there's a guy who says, 'I was with Custer at Little Big Horn.' When you read that on the page, you can maintain the value of that fantasy, because you know he was a garrulous old Indian who probably was never at Little Big Horn. But when you show, in a picture, the event, there's no way you can talk the audience into believing he wasn't at Little Big Horn, because you've *seen* him." Referring to the people depicted in *Alice's Restaurant,* he adds, "Sure, they had a few parties, but not like the one at the end of the movie. So these things merge like you wouldn't believe. Often after they are shown in the picture, the actual people who were depicted in life begin to believe that what we showed in the picture was real. The actual people start to believe what they saw in the movie."

If you speak to the friends who were featured in the film, invariably they will tell you that it was completely untrue, but if you ask what it was really like, they will recount events that sound very similar, if not identical, to the film. What is misleading about the movie, they say, is not so much the events it recounts but the point it tries to make about those events. More scenes were based on real-life events than were pure works of fiction. Yet, for those people the film depicted, the inclusion of fictional scenes conspired to give the real-life events a different meaning than they'd had.

"There's a scene in the movie, for example," Arlo says, "where I pat Pat Quinn, who plays Alice, on the butt, as if I were that familiar with Alice, the real Alice, which of course was total fiction. I never had any relationship with Alice other than just a normal being-a-friend. So when the movie came out people said, 'Oh, see, we knew Arlo had something going with Alice.' When everybody is using their real names or just appearing as themselves in a movie based on a real incident, everyone assumes everything else is true also."

The film featured a scene in which the church bell fills the night with its resonant chime. When Arlo asks his on-screen girlfriend about it, she replies, referring to owners Ray and Alice, "It's an ancient custom of the manor — the lord and lady ring the bell after they make it."

This "fact" was later repeated in an issue of *Life* magazine, but Alice insists such a "custom" never existed at her manor. "We were aware we had neighbors," she says simply. "We rang it once or twice, but it was a massive bell. I was afraid it was going to come down. You don't want to yank it too much."

"The movie kind of ran parallel to the truth, and used some of the same people, but it just wasn't like that," Alice continues. "I never had sexual relations of any kind with Arlo Guthrie — or any of those kids. I was a mother figure. We never shot heroin or anything like that. We were horrified by that. We smoked pot. I went crazy when I saw that. Nothing is quite true. Arthur wanted to make a statement. I'm sure *Bonnie and Clyde* wasn't terribly accurate either. It was romanticized. You had to have sex and drugs and rock and roll, and you have to have violence. That scene where Arlo gets beat up — people with long hair did get beat up, but I don't think Arlo did. I couldn't tell you what wasn't true. It just wasn't true. That was not Arthur Penn's concern. He just wanted to capture the time, and we were just stand-ins for Hippie USA. The generic hippies."

As Alice and Ray were like the blast furnace of the Van Deusenville community, the movie *Alice's Restaurant* was like the closure of that furnace. It was an unforseen event that marked the beginning of the end for this particular church community.

"By the time the movie came out there is not one relationship that lasted that was going on at the time before the movie was made," Arlo recalls. "Everybody became separated, divorced, or went their separate ways or still have not spoken to each other, mostly because of what the reaction of the local community was to all of these people. A lot of lives were ruined. A lot of relationships were ruined. I wouldn't say as the result of the film, but the film was the catalyst. If something was weak, the film acted as the final straw that broke it. There was nothing strong enough to withstand it in terms of a relationship. By the end of the movie

Ray and Alice weren't together, so we were filming the movie of them breaking up while they were actually breaking up in real life, with all their friends there to see it. Both on the film and real life. It was an incredibly painful, difficult time. I think the result was, at the end of the movie, everyone had had enough of each other. Anytime you work with anybody for a long period of time under difficult circumstances, you've had enough after a while, so all these friends went their separate ways. And of course with the fame and fortune I received as a result of it, that also changed a lot of friendships because a lot of people didn't know how to deal with that — because they didn't know how to deal with me as a famous person and they didn't know how to relate to me as just who I'd always been. They couldn't acknowledge that I was famous, but at the same time they couldn't lie and say I wasn't, so they were put in this dilemma of not knowing how to act. Here you are friends with someone for a long time and someone comes up to them and treats them like God, how are you supposed to react? You're not going to treat them like God. You almost want to make sure that they're not, and so you do things to bring somebody down to your own size. If you're the person who happens to be God at that moment, it's not really fun to have people bringing you down all the time to reassure them of what their relationships are. So the movie created an atmosphere of disillusion, just as it had in the script, which was written before anything was dissolved. It was life imitating art."

To many observers it seemed that everything that had existed before the movie was reversed by the time it ended. "It was very strange," says a local resident. "You had Obie, who arrested Arlo and hated the hippies — now he and Arlo were buddies. Obie was on the street signing autographs for the hippies, and Arlo was up on a farm putting up a fence for privacy."

Alice didn't blame the movie for the disbanding of the community. In 1972 she told *Berkshire Eagle* reporter Arthur Myers, "I don't think the movie broke up the group. By the time the movie was shot, our lives had already changed. Lives are always changing, especially when you're in your teens and twenties. So I can't say the movie was responsible for breaking up the old gang any more than graduation is responsible for breaking up a high school gang. If you have a real basis for friendship, things like that don't change it."

But fame did have its effects. Everyone reacted to it in his or her own way. Geoff Outlaw, for example, says he took acting classes in case any more film opportunities presented themselves. He now lives in Texas and says people to this day recognize him from the movie. "It was a phenomenal experience, and it keeps going on."

He says Arlo was not changed by his fame. "He's exactly the same as he was in fourth grade," he says. "Except that his hair is grayer. He has not changed a lick in all these years. And most of the people that we were friendly with are still the same too. There hasn't been a degeneration of humor or a lack of fun in people's lives even though we've all had our ups and downs over the years."

For Tina Chen and some of the other professional actors, the recognition was rewarding. "I've done things where I have much more interesting parts," she says. "In this film I was just tagging along, but being able to work with Arthur Penn and being with Alice and that crowd — it was part of an institution in some ways. I think in retrospect I realize it had much bigger impact than I realized when I was there. It was just, for me, the beginning of being a working filmmaker. It was a lot of our first films, and that's why it was special for a lot of us. We had fun because it was a whole group of young people. They are fond memories."

For Alice, fame was, and continues to be, a mixed blessing. It brought her some opportunities but prevented others from coming to fruition. In the wake of the movie she wrote a cookbook and went on tour promoting both film and book for about a year and a half. She appeared on talk shows like *Merv Griffin*. The *Alice's Restaurant Cookbook* sold between 55,000 and 70,000 copies and has become a sought-after collectible. On the other hand, Alice found the promotional schedule grueling and finally stopped when she was plagued by splitting headaches.

"Most reporters wanted to know how many lovers I'd had while I was married," she says. "No one ever asked me for a recipe."

Although Ray Brock's name recognition as a result of the film was much lower than Alice's, he also used the publicity as a springboard for his books — children's books on how to build things, with titles like *You Can Build a Table and a Chair Too*. Unfortunately, fame had few lasting benefits for him. In the words of Paul Kleinwald, "Ray had demons chasing him, and he was just not able to conquer them."

"The church was no longer in existence after the movie," Rick Robbins says. "Ray and Alice were no longer together. Their relationship was gone. Ray somehow started to slip, and he got worse and worse over the years. He had a problem with drinking, and he really dropped out. In the early years he was somebody that was so strong and so creative and so energized and incredibly well read, had a great voice, great guitar player, singer, artist. He could draw this room. Then Ray slowly got worse and worse. He stopped being so creative. He got further and further down the road to alcoholism and stopped taking care of himself. It was really a shame. We still loved him. But we were wondering who was going to take care of him."

Ray had never been very good with money. Once, Alice recalls, she and Ray were sitting down for dinner at the church when the power went out. She yelled at him, "I can't believe you didn't pay the electric bill!" Ray looked at her sheepishly, assuming that it was his fault. It wasn't until they got to a restaurant that they realized the entire area had suffered a blackout.

By December 1969, the church was on the brink of foreclosure. Alice's Restaurant, Inc., of which Alice was a shareholder, considered converting the church into a restaurant. Alice's association with the corporation, which wanted to franchise Alice's Restaurants, was brief. She says she was unaware of their plan to buy the church. Although to this day many people assume there was an Alice's Restaurant in the church, there never was. When the issue came up before the zoning board, about fifty people showed up to object to a variance that would allow the corporation to put a business there. The neighbors complained about potential noise, traffic problems, and, of course, garbage. One neighbor called the application "a sham to flout the zoning bylaw."

Attorney John Dwyer said a restaurant would bring considerable profit to the area. He said that otherwise the building was likely to "always be a run-down former church." In the face of vigorous opposition, however, he withdrew the proposal. Eventually the church was sold to Attorney Seymour Barash of Freeport, New York, for $21,000.

Alice did open a new restaurant, just not in the church. Her book, *My Life as a Restaurant*, chronicles the day-to-day operations at the roadside establishment. "One day in February of 1971 I realized I was broke," she wrote. "I had had a good time, but it was over, and it was time to come up with a new life. I drove around thinking, 'A restaurant

— oh, God, has it come to that?'"

The new restaurant was called "Take Out Alice." It was housed in the former Furnace Package Store in a residential section of Stockbridge, which Alice described as "a lopsided wooden shack that sold beer, wine, potato chips, cigarettes, soda, and stuff like that." After less than a year of successful take-out operation, Alice wanted to expand the business by adding outdoor seating and a license to sell alcohol. She found herself constantly at odds with the town selectmen over the various variances. The discussions were often heated and always made headlines. At one point Alice walked out of a meeting of the selectmen. In 1975 *Berkshire Eagle* reporter Milton Bass referred to the business as a place where Alice "serves the public dinners seven days a week, and battles the selectmen twice a month." Alice publicly accused the selectmen of "harassing" her.

"They wanted her out," said a local resident. "It was just ugly. You just got the impression they didn't want her there. She had a lot of unconventional friends, and it was a conservative town. The actual dispute was not really that important."

The selectmen denied the charges. "At no time has Alice been treated any differently from anyone else in the town," said selectman James F. Kiley.

Eventually she tired of the battles and closed the takeout. She next opened an upscale restaurant/resort called Alice's at Avaloch. Its elegant dining room featured linen tablecloths and crystal. She soon found herself embroiled in another battle, however, this one over the type of sewer system she planned to install. The business did not survive. In 1979 she closed the restaurant and filed for bankruptcy. She decided to leave the Berkshires and start a new life elsewhere that would not include running a restaurant.

That same year, Ray Brock passed away. Shortly before his death, friends say, he was getting his life back together. He had returned to Virginia, where he married his high school sweetheart and worked as a self-employed boat builder. He died of a heart attack while sailing on Chesapeake Bay in a ship he had built himself. He was fifty.

Alice moved to Provincetown, where she says she has been "sort of a hermit." Eventually she bought a house on the ocean with a downstairs apartment she rents to vacationers. The advertisement for the house said it included "a private chapel." She took that as a sign. The former chapel now serves as Alice's studio, where she paints and draws. She has

GERARD MALANGA

Ray and Alice Brock in front of Take Out Alice, around 1973.

illustrated two books, including a children's book, *Mooses Come Walking,* written by Arlo Guthrie. Most recently she's been working on decorative illustrations with a kitchen theme. She says she would like to sell more of her work in the future. She has mixed feelings about her *Alice's Restaurant* fame. She has moved on and says she doesn't want to keep reliving one period of her life, especially a period that was, in many ways, personally difficult. On the other hand, the foyer that leads to her guest apartment is decorated with framed photos of her famous past life. "People like to see them," she says with a shrug.

Ultimately she likes the power she has to bring people joy just by being *that* Alice. "People come up and ask me for my autograph. I find it hard to say no to them because it makes them so happy. They're thrilled to meet Alice of *Alice's Restaurant.* I'm a symbol of something that was meaningful to them."

The old church in Housatonic was no longer the center of the community that it had been when the movie was made and released. For a while, friends hung out there with Ray. They remember swinging across the sanctuary on ropes the film crew had left behind. It wasn't long, however, before the church was sold. The kids were getting older now, too, and they were finding their place in the world, getting married, and building homes of their own.

"When the movie ended, I was left feeling empty and sad, and that feeling for me was true," Paul Kleinwald says. "There was a lot of turmoil at the same time there were a lot of interesting things going on."

Many viewers, including critic Robert Hatch, were left with the impression that "young people today — those, that is, who make up what might be called the movement — are willing to travel light and uncommitted. Relationships have depth but not much length, and when the vibrations falter, there is always another scene down the road."

The people who were at "Alice's Church" in its heyday, however, insist that it was not the failed dream of a Utopian commune that the movie makes it out to be. Unlike their film counterparts, these young people were not a movement or a symbol of anything; they were simply a group of friends. As with any group, some friendships proved to be enduring and others fell away. Some weathered the storms of life; others were sunk by them. While Arlo lost a number of acquaintances after the film, he says his core group of friends are still his friends to this day. The relationships that had depth also had length.

But it was time for the next chapter in the lives of the "church people," and the next chapter in the life of the church.

"What do you have that's eccentric, with lots of space?"

— Artist Ellen Lanyon

Great Barrington, 1970

O ver the next two decades fashions changed. Clothing of natural fibers was replaced by colorful synthetics; long straight hair was cut into styles requiring lots of spray and mousse. The adults were no longer telling Arlo to cut his hair . . . his kids were. Folk music became a rarity on the radio, replaced by disco and New Wave. Warner Brothers, Arlo's record label, did its best to rid itself of its less profitable, folk-inspired artists. The number of pilgrims to the site of the Massacree declined, although it never dropped off completely.

Although the final image of the film *Alice's Restaurant* was dark and somber, most fans recall the movie as upbeat, even fun. (Most video rental stores, in fact, file *Alice's Restaurant* with their comedy titles.) Viewers did not see the church as the setting of a broken marriage, a young man who dies of a heroin overdose, or the failed dream of a commune. What they remembered were the scenes in which the church was full of people singing, playing music, and feeling free to be whatever they wanted in each other's presence. Long after the details of the movie had been forgotten, fans remembered those images and wished they had a place like that, a place based on the real Brock church/home but made even better by its transfer to the big screen.

"Most people wanted to see what the church looked like as a result of hearing the record, and they used the movie for that," Arlo says. "They didn't want to fall into the darkness of the movie itself. Its lasting impression wasn't the movie; the lasting impression was the song. Having seen the movie, you could put the song in a visual context. For most people, seeing the movie was enough, and some of them still come and just want to see it."

Thirty years later, Lisa Jackson, a longtime Arlo fan from Amarillo, Texas, confirms this theory. She says she can't remember the ending of the movie at all, although she still remembers the film fondly. "The movie came out, I was sixteen or seventeen. The whole concept behind the movie is wonderful because our boyfriends and brothers and people were being sent overseas to Vietnam. It was a scary time and we didn't agree with the concept of the war, and I had friends that did crazy things to try to keep from being drafted. I mean, one guy I knew shot his foot. There were some that were heading for Canada. The whole story behind *Alice's Restaurant* is funny. This guy got arrested for littering and they didn't think he was good enough to go kill people. You can't help but just love the whole concept. The Vietnam War, the draft thing, was a serious matter. The movie wasn't making light of it, but they were showing how ridiculous the government can be. His humor is so dry and yet it doesn't harm anyone. There are a lot of comedians who are cruel. With the movie, of course, you have the visuals, and Arlo, he's always been kind of a cute thing. Even my eighty-year-old mother thinks he's adorable, and she doesn't agree with our politics or anything like that."

So people kept coming to see the church to try to recapture the positive feelings they remembered from the film. During the 1970s and '80s a number of artists were drawn to the church as well. The combination of vast space and rich cultural history made it the perfect site for an artistic endeavor. Perhaps only an artist would buy a building like the church — beautiful and historic, but almost entirely impractical.

Tenants envisioned studios, theaters, and galleries in its belly, but they often left quickly after they discovered the town's reluctance to allow any type of business in the R-2 (low-density) residential zone. There

JUDY BEISLER

was little evidence left that Division Street and Route 41 had once been a busy industrial crossroads with a train depot, hotel, and iron works. The street had become entirely residential and quiet, and the neighbors wanted to keep it that way.

The first person to own the building after the Brocks was an attorney named Seymour Barash. When he bought the place, it had been empty for three weeks. Ray had left for the West Coast, and "transient young people" had taken up residence there. Barash described the property as "extremely filthy inside," but he told a *Berkshire Eagle* reporter it was still attractive. "It's part of today's generation, and it's still a beautiful church. No kidding, I feel religious just standing inside it, and I'm not a religious man."

Barash put a caretaker family in the building to protect his investment and spent about $4,000 to repair the roof, ceiling, and walls. His plan was to sell it back to the town. He felt the church was part of local history and therefore should be used as a town museum, library, or municipal building.

Alice had a more skeptical view of his motives. "He's probably going to exploit it for more money," she told the *Berkshire Eagle*. "Going to stick some of his own beatniks in there and make even more money. He just isn't my type of person."

Coincidentally, the spot on Prospect Hill where the famous dumping incident took place was also sold at this time. The new owner, Mrs. Fanny P. Cullerton, built a home there.

Great Barrington rejected Seymour Barash's proposal. Over the next few years he rented the property to a number of artists. There was Larry Ennis, proprietor of the Art Union in Lenox, who planned to open an art gallery and a school to teach painting, pottery, and sculpture. The sanctuary was used as a gallery by the Art Union for only one summer. Next, three theater men, John Parriott of Lenox and Timothy Oppee and Richard Howell of New York, proposed to use the space to produce original plays they hoped would go on to Broadway. They felt that the pressures of New York City were not conducive to good theater and wanted to start their own repertory company, based in the church, with four or five actors. The same old problems — residential zoning, lack of parking space, and neighbors' objections — prevented this dream from becoming reality.

There *was* some activity in the church, though. The sanctuary was briefly the site of a monthly program of English country dancing. The first Friday of every month, musicians, a dance caller, and sixty or seventy dancers would gather and have a good time.

In 1975 Janet and Steve Voorhees moved into the church, which they rented for $200 a month. As *Berkshire Eagle* reporter Stephen Fay wrote, "A disheartening accumulation of plaster, leaves and assorted offal greeted the new tenants." They installed shelves and a woodburning stove and turned the bell tower into a home again. They wanted to do more to restore the church, which was beginning to look decidedly tired.

"Unfortunately," Steve Voorhees told Fay, "my financial foundation collapsed at about the same time the church's foundation caved in."

Two years later Seymour Barash sold the church for $39,000 to

William Schlesinger, who had founded the art and advertising department of the City University of New York. An artist who painted corporate murals, Schlesinger planned to entirely remodel the church with the help of his daughter, Shari, an architect; his wife, an interior designer; and architect Steven Robinson. He said the design would em-phasize the "wonderful panorama" of the church's interior but would entail no changes to the exterior. He said he would "keep the architectural integrity of the building."

One change was made to the exterior, however. When they were working on the roof, they removed the wooden crosses that had stood on each of the roof's points. The 111-year-old crosses were presented to Canon Middleton, who put them in the basement of the St. James Church "until a museum or other suitable display site is established." One of the crosses found its way into the woodpile of a neighbor, Les Davis, who

AMY FELD

The church as it appeared in the 1980s, with both doors replaced by windows.

would later become a valued friend of the Guthrie Center. He gave the cross to the center, where it is now on display inside the church.

The designers tried to overcome one of the building's greatest drawbacks, the cost of heating the sanctuary, while simultaneously enlarging the living space. They extended the living room halfway into the former sanctuary, thus creating a heated cell and a vast unheated area that included the now-smaller sanctuary as well as a loft under the rose window that extended into the sanctuary from where the choir loft had once been. They also broke through the wall on that level to the bell tower, allowing access to the tower's top two floors from the loft.

The living area was outfitted with dark paneling and a Gothic arch motif. The newly installed kitchen was state of the art. As with previous owners, some of Schlesinger's more ambitious plans were never realized. He planned to install solar heating but did not. An even grander scheme was to operate an art gallery in the sanctuary to show and sell the work of regional artists. He would bring people up from New York City on buses for art and a meal cooked in his elaborate kitchen. Once again the town selectmen refused to grant a zoning variance.

Since Schlesinger couldn't operate a business in a building that was so expensive to maintain, he didn't want it. The church was up for sale again. Around this time Roland Ginzel and Ellen Lanyon, artists from Illinois, were looking to relocate to the East. They hoped to find a unique home and turned to their son's wife, a real estate agent in northern Connecticut. They asked her, "What do you have that's eccentric, with lots of space?" She knew just the place.

They came out to visit for the Thanksgiving holiday and on Thanksgiving Day went to see the property. Neither artist was familiar with *Alice's Restaurant* or the building's fame. They didn't know until later that there was any significance to visiting on Thanksgiving. They knew who Woody Guthrie was, but not Arlo. They saw in the sanctuary a perfect artist's studio and bought it right away.

When the couple moved in, they found several boxes of broken glass in the basement — remnants of the stained-glass windows. Some of the patterned pieces were complete, and the artists made window decorations with them. They gave two flower-shaped panels to their neighbor, Mary Sachs. Only one stained-glass window remained in the building, the round rose window with its depictions of Matthew, Mark, Luke, and John.

"The rose window was so beautiful," Ellen says. "We had a bed up there in the unheated section. We would have guests there in the summer. They said it was fantastic to wake up in the morning and have the light shining in on them."

The studio was also in the unheated portion of the church, so they were able to use it each year until about Thanksgiving. "I felt an enormous contentment there," Ellen says. "I'm not a country girl, so I never had experienced the quiet. I did some very good painting there. It was almost spiritual to be there."

It was also a little weird. One evening Roland sat down in his living room to watch television. When he turned on the set, there on the screen was a picture of the room in which he was sitting. The station was showing *Alice's Restaurant*.

There were also a fair number of uninvited guests to the church. Most would just stand on the front lawn and have their pictures taken in front of the building, but others peered in the windows. Some went even further.

"People would just walk in," Ellen says. "I'd be painting and I'd turn and they'd just be standing there. People used to knock on the door and want to buy things. They rang the doorbell at two or three in the morning."

Eventually Ellen and Roland put a sign out front that said PRIVATE RESIDENCE to keep people from just walking in. But usually, if visitors knocked on the door at a reasonable hour, they were happy to show them around.

"People that came to the door with long hair would point up to the bell tower and say, 'I lived up there,'" Roland recalls.

Ellen, now well aware of the song "Alice's Restaurant," finally heard the whole thing one day while she was painting the church and had the radio on. She understood then why it had been so popular. She was surprised by how interesting it was.

By 1990 the pair had decided to sell the building. It was simply too big and too expensive to heat and maintain. While they were preparing to put it on the market, they received a telephone call from Arlo Guthrie's office. A Boston television station was filming a show called "Whatever Happened To . . ." and one of the episodes was going to feature Arlo Guthrie. The producers wanted to know if they could shoot a segment with the musician playing a song on the church lawn. They said they would not come inside. The couple agreed. The television crew showed up and went about their business with little disruption. As they were packing up to go, Roland and Ellen noticed a man with long white hair peeking in their windows.

Arlo Guthrie, 1992.

JUDY BEISLER

"You have a relationship with places just like you have with people, and you have obligations that come and hit you in the face, and you can't just walk away because it's not convenient. You have to deal with it."

— Arlo Guthrie

Great Barrington, 1990

T he man was, of course, Arlo Guthrie. It had been nearly eighteen years since he had been in the church, and he just had to take a look inside. It had changed quite a bit, but it was definitely the same place, and the feeling was still there for him. The Ginzels invited Arlo inside and gave him a tour. Then they all sat down and had coffee. Arlo told them he had written at least twenty songs in the building.

"The place was really a part of his life. He got all sentimental," Roland says.

And what did "ever happen to Arlo" in those eighteen years? Quite a bit, in fact. At forty-three, Arlo was still married to Jackie Hyde, the stately California girl he'd wed in an oh-so-sixties ceremony in October 1969. They were the parents of four children and grandparents of one — their son Abe's son.

Arlo met Jackie in Los Angeles at the Troubadour Club, where he was performing and she was working as a waitress. Jackie, who once said she'd had a premonition about meeting Arlo, was at the club only by chance. She had been camping by herself in the Baja Peninsula when her car broke down. She'd managed to hitch a ride back to the Troubadour so she could make enough money to go back to the camp, fix her car, and stay for another six months. Instead, she met the man who, she says, reminded her of "a European prince." Friends say the couple was immediately inseparable. They were married three months later.

The wedding took place outdoors on 250 acres of Berkshire meadow. The fall colors were at their peak on the bright, sunny day at the foot of a hill between two little red houses. About 150 guests attended, including Ray Brock, Judy Collins, Stacy Keach, producer Hillard Elkins, Claire Bloom, and Officer Obie. There were also a number of uninvited guests, members of the press who wanted to record the events of the day. Guests from New York arrived by bus. Marjorie Guthrie, the first off the bus, said, "I feel like a flower child." To which Arlo replied, "You look like a flower child."

So did the bride and groom, both dressed in outfits of the same white silk and both with identical white flowers in their hair. Jackie was dressed in a high-waisted, full-length gown. Arlo wore bell-bottom pants and a matching shirt and vest. Geoff Outlaw was the best man, and the bride's sister, Nita Hyde, was the maid of honor. The guests' clothes "ranged from traditional to see-through blouses, ponchos, Levi's, and hand-embroidered Mexican wedding shirts," wrote one of the uninvited guests. "The hippie types seemed to outnumber the squares."

Alice cooked all the food for the Guthrie wedding. The tables were laden with lasagne, roast beef, turkey, Alice's famous shrimp, and lots of champagne and punch.

Judy Collins sang "Suzanne," and Marjorie read a poem written by Woody that she had saved for the event. "May your gladness ripen as a yellow sweet fruit," it said. "May you never include the word 'enemy' in your vocabulary. May you attain."

The couple exchanged traditional vows. After the justice of the peace, Donald Feder, pronounced the couple man and wife, Arlo led the guests in singing "Amazing Grace." Bill Obanhein kissed the bride. He put his arm around the groom and said, "Congratulations, my friend, but I don't think I'll kiss you." Following the wedding, the newlyweds left for a concert tour.

Their son, Abraham, was born in April 1970, followed by Cathy in 1972, Annie in 1976, and Sarah in 1980. In 1972 Arlo had his first and only full-fledged chart hit with Steve Goodman's "City of New Orleans," which peaked at number eighteen on the Billboard charts on October 28 of that year. For a while he was releasing about an album a year, always touring and playing music. He later described this time in his newsletter, the *Rolling Blunder Review:* "1975 through 1985 became family years . . . We settled into whatever family life we could make and still be on the road. It was a little crazy, but everyone seemed to come through intact."

Then the '80s happened. Of course, from Arlo's point of view, there never really was a '70s.

"The '70s never really existed," he once said. "Many people are unaware that the '60s actually began in 1965 and continued until 1974. The '70s started in 1975, but then disco came along and that was it. Now the '80s were the Reagan years. He defined that time in history for good or ill. My friends around the world told me there was no way we'd elect him. I said we'd elect him any way we could. We love to have actors in the White House."

Professionally, the Big '80s were tough on folksingers. The collective culture of the decade was concerned with making money, looking glamorous, and appearing wealthier, more beautiful, and more successful than everyone else. Synthesizers and drum machines operated by men wearing thick makeup were in; simple songs with social themes were out. Arlo's record label, Warner Brothers, dropped Arlo and other artists such as Gordon Lightfoot and Bonnie Raitt in favor of Devo, the B-52s, and the Talking Heads. Arlo called it the "Purge of 1982."

In 1983, when the last of several five-album contracts had expired, Arlo completed an album called "Someday" and delivered it to Warner Brothers. They didn't like it but said they'd release it anyway. Considering the amount of promotion they had done on recent albums they *had* liked, this did not sound promising at all. Arlo convinced Warner to let him release the album on his own newly formed label, Rising Son Records. Surprisingly, as they had spent $75,000 to produce "Someday," they let Arlo have it. He also convinced Warner to give him a dozen other albums they no longer listed in their catalog. "Alice's Restaurant," which was still selling, they kept.

"I got control of my work because no one else wanted it," Arlo told *Acoustic Guitar* magazine. "But it ended up being a very smart and fortunate move. There's a big difference between a small independent record label and a big corporate giant. The major corporate giants need to make a profit. Individuals don't. So we started our own record company in 1983 with this fact in mind. If we could employ one or two or three people in the world, have more Arlo records on the street from one day to the next, be able to make records consistently, and not lose any money, we were ahead of the game."

Rising Son Records began modestly, with Arlo, Jackie, and a few friends working out of their Washington, Massachusetts, home. They had two houses — the main house, where everybody lived, and the lower house, which became a guest house and office. The one or two staff members would walk into a kitchen area, then up a couple of steps into what would have been a dining area but was now full of papers and computers and files. On one side was a living room, and upstairs were bedrooms.

"It was interesting working there when they had guests, because the guests would stay there," says Sharon Palma, former manager of Rising Son. "Ramblin' Jack Elliot came a lot. Hoyt Axton was there one day. It was like being in somebody's house."

The Guthries compiled a mailing list by typing the names and addresses of people who had signed up at concerts into a computer database. Once they had that, they planned to send out an announcement, which would later evolve into a "sometimes quarterly" newsletter called the *Rolling Blunder Review.*

The plan got off to an inauspicious start. After they had typed in more than six thousand addresses, the computer asked Jackie if she wanted to "initialize" the program. She said yes, pushed the button, and the entire list of names was erased, forcing the group to begin from scratch. Fortunately, Jackie had just printed out the labels, which they used to send out a mailing explaining the situation. The first proper, single-sheet mailing was sent out in 1986. It advertised the availability of three of Arlo's albums.

"These records are only available on cassette tapes, for now," it said. "At some time in the future we may decide to grow them on regular record stuff. But being our own record company (these days), and not having as many options, we decided to grow some high-quality, real-time recorded, chrome type tapes, instead of the regular scratchy kind of records. They are available at present only through the mail (see return address) or at the shows."

In the next mailing, Arlo added: "Some folks have been asking about when we are going to put out regular records, instead of cassettes. The answer is 'We're not,' at least not yet. Too expensive now. The plan is to get out all the albums we've done over the years on tape first. Then, if there are enough of you really interested, we'll start putting out regular records. Of course by then they may be obsolete. It's nice just to have all the stuff becoming available again."

It was an accurate prediction. Eventually most of Arlo's back catalog was available through Rising Son on cassettes and newfangled CDs.

It took six or seven years to get the business on its feet, and the process required all of Arlo's attention. "The records were doing well, but I looked around one day and I hadn't written any new songs," he told a reporter. "I said, hmmm, what's wrong with this picture? I might as well have put on a suit and tie and forget about it. But the business part wasn't bad or anything. I did discover that I had some creative abilities in that way too."

By 1990 the business was fully operational. A growing number of fans were keeping in touch with the folksinger thanks to the *Rolling Blunder Review*. They dubbed themselves "Blunderites" and thought nothing of traveling across several states to see Arlo Guthrie's annual Carnegie Hall Thanksgiving concert. His photo was no longer on the cover of *Esquire* or *Newsweek*, but, as Arlo put it, "despite dwindling crowds and a rude awakening from Warner Brothers, we kept touring," and thousands of people across the country were reading about Arlo four times (roughly) a year. Now that they knew in advance where he was playing, more fans started showing up at his concerts and buying his music.

As the business became more successful, it became less practical to keep it in the Guthrie household. "People were coming up there all the time, and we had no privacy anymore," Arlo says. "There were always FedEx trucks coming up every day, UPS every day. Everyone knew where we were, so our farm wasn't private."

Although in the back of his mind he knew it would be good to move the office, Arlo had not made any concrete plans to do so, and until he went to shoot the segment of "Whatever Happened To . . ." he had thought little about the church. He had not returned there since the movie had been shot. It had certainly never crossed his mind to buy it. Even when he saw the place again, purchasing the property was the farthest thing from his mind.

"I thought it was horrible what had happened to it," he recalls. "It had such an incredible beauty to it, and a simplicity to it, and it was obvious that a lot of people had been through there that didn't have any skills of preserving the beauty of the thing. All the stained glass was gone except the rose window, and that was in disrepair. All of the stuff that Ray had built and the simple, almost Shaker-like beauty was all ripped out and gone. It was turned into this sort of monstrous thing that looks like a pueblo inside of a ship, and nothing really worked. It was functionally ridiculous and unsound. Now there were leaks where there hadn't been before because someone had put a roof in the wrong place. The paint was peeling off, the windows were shot, everything was falling down. You could tell that people had spent money in there, but on the stupid stuff. They put money into making nice walls, but nobody put any money into the sills or the structure, so the result was that the whole place was falling down — but the bedroom was nice. It was ridiculously spent money, people just looking to be somebody. They weren't concerned about the church itself. Even so, with all those problems, it still had a kind of quiet magic to it. But I had no desire to be in there or to possess it in that sense. I just thought it was a great old building."

When he went in and talked with the Ginzels, however, the opportunity presented itself. Sitting in the kitchen with the couple, Arlo felt a touch of nostalgia. "I wish I owned this place," he said.

"Well, as a matter of fact, we're selling it," Ellen replied. She remembers the moment as "kind of a spiritual transition of events."

Arlo rushed back to the office full of energy. "We're buying the church!" The office staff was skeptical. "We've got to do this," he said. "This has got to happen."

"Arlo came up with these fabulous ideas," Sharon Palma says, "some of which you knew could never come to fruition and others seemed like they might be possible. This one seemed like it might be possible. It was exciting."

Contrary to popular belief, "rich" and "famous" do not always go together, certainly not to the extent one might imagine. Although Arlo's business was doing well and he was by no means impoverished, he was basically a working guy with a family to feed, and he didn't have an extra $350,000 (later lowered to $300,000) in his jeans pocket.

"The opportunity was there to buy it, but I knew I couldn't afford to," Arlo says. "I had already taken on financial responsibilities that I was borderline going to survive anyway. Plus they wanted about three hundred thousand for this thing, which was about a hundred thousand over what it was valued at, so you couldn't even go to the bank. So I said I'd take it on if I could do it, but it didn't matter to me. I wasn't on a mission from God at this point. On the other hand, I also knew that there were still people coming from all over the world who were stopping and taking their picture there, and obviously it was all related to the film and to the record. It turns out that those works — I didn't know it at the time--they changed people's lives at a time when not much funny was going on. I thought if there's something we can do for all the people for whom this means something, we had to do it." So he turned to his subscribers for suggestions on how to buy it.

CHURCH FOR SALE

The church in which folksinger Arlo Guthrie first began to write and sing "The Alice's Restaurant Massacree" is for sale. Guthrie met with the present owners during the summer of 1990 and made the discovery of the pending sale at that time. Since then the folksinger has been wondering what he could do, if anything, to save the building from becoming inaccessible (as it has been all these years) to those interested in visiting the site where the movie *Alice's Restaurant* was filmed . . .

The church, which is still in pretty good condition, has been changed somewhat over the years, but much of the old feelings can still be felt: there is STILL something there.

Guthrie is contemplating whether or not to set up a fund for the acquisition of the building. A kind of "Save The Church" fund could be used to raise monies from contributors for the purpose of buying the building. Arlo noted that while the church wasn't actually going to fall or be torn down in the immediate future, the possible eventuality of such a catastrophe was as good as any other possible future.

"If we don't take advantage of the ability to buy it now, we will almost certainly be at a disadvantage if we wish to do so in the future. The cost of the building has been set at $350,000, and we are going to try to raise that amount as quickly as possible."

There may be ways, other than a fund type of idea, to accomplish the task, so Guthrie is listening to anyone who may have ideas on the subject. Readers with good ideas, or who have recently won a lottery and wish to contribute, should write. Please don't send money, just ideas!

The folksinger noted that while some of his ideas are reasonable, there are many that fall short of reason. That is why nothing has yet been organized. Guthrie's long time friend and producer, John Pilla, who passed away recently, noted that Guthrie was 10% genius and 90% crazy.

"That may be true," said Guthrie. "The problem is to determine which of the ideas fall into the 10% category and which fall into the 90%."

Arlo's call for ideas was fruitful. Hundreds of letters came in. Some of the suggestions were impractical, some fanciful, but a few were useful. Among them, the idea of forming a nonprofit organization appealed to Arlo, not only for financial reasons but also because of his personal desire to work for social causes. Turning the church into a real force for good in the community seemed the ideal fate for the landmark.

"I thought it would be nice to keep some of the spiritual aspect, because after all it was a church," he says. "There were still local people who had gone there as young people. I thought it would be nice for them to celebrate the basic spirituality of the building without making it a particular variety. Just letting them know that in some way the history of the building would be maintained for what it really was and not for what all these people had used it for. I thought it would be good to put in there some of what I was interested in, some of the charitable stuff that we do anyway and had been doing for years, if we could put it all under one roof. When people call me up and say, 'Are you going to do this benefit, save this and farm that,' I could get it organized and I could organize my own time by having a crew who did that permanently. That really didn't work out. It's a little scattered, but the organizations are in place."

He took the best of the ideas his fans had submitted to his lawyer and accountants. They told him not to do it. Arlo thought their advice was good — and decided not to take it.

"I said, 'You don't understand. I don't *want* to, I *have* to do it,'" he explains. "You have a relationship with places just like you have with people, and you have obligations that come and hit you in the face, and you can't just walk away because it's not convenient. You have to deal with it. And although it's been a mess for us financially for a long time — I mean it virtually stopped everything we wanted to do — we took on a burden with the hope that we could pull it off. I didn't wait to see what would happen. I just went ahead and did it anyway."

At the time he had few specific ideas about what good deeds the center would perform. Those details would be worked out later, as he went along. He had a broad concept, however. The center would be locally based and focused, it would be open to everyone who wanted to take part, and it would be guided, as Arlo himself was, by the principles of his guru, Ma Jaya Bhagavati, a Jewish woman from Brooklyn who had taken the Indian name as part of her rebirth as a Hindu spiritual advisor. The mission of the nonprofit organization was vague by design, Arlo says.

"A lot of people, when they set up an organization to save the world, are convinced that if you only do what I know, everything will be fine. If you only save those whales, the whole world will be fine. If you just save those trees . . . Everybody has a plan to save the world. If you're a person in my shoes, you've seen a lot of plans, and a lot of people in the world still aren't saved. You've got to save yourself before you can save the world. If you can't save yourself, you can't save the world. So I thought it would be nice to have a place where you can save yourself, or at least get your act together, and the best way of doing that that I know of is helping someone else. It doesn't actually benefit you personally, but it does in the long run because when you put yourself aside you learn the benefits of putting yourself aside, which I think are invaluable tools to making the world a better place. So we wanted to set up an organization that would be able to respond to the needs of people in the area."

The town of Great Barrington, on the other hand, was not satisfied with that answer. They wanted to know exactly what services the organization would provide and a detailed plan of how it intended to provide them.

"Well, that's just another guy with another plan to save the world," Arlo muses. "We've got thousands of those organizations in this area alone. If I knew [what the community needed] I would just go do that. What I want to do is be *responsive*. It means I don't know in advance what needs to be done. What I want to do is set up something where, if somebody needs something, they can call up and say, 'I need this,' and I'll have a group of volunteers and say, 'Who can take care of this?' And someone will say, 'I can.' If we don't know anybody, we'll say, 'Well, who can find out about it?' Someone will say, 'I can,' and we'll find out about it. If we can't, we'll say, 'We're sorry, we can't do nothing.' Simple, honest, direct. They didn't want to hear about it. They wanted to hear how many people are going to be there, are you going to have services, what are the services, what are you going to say, who's going to come, what's going to happen. So I had to make up some preliminary ideas on what we were going to do. We had to choose some things that were closest to our ability to deal with, and we formed two not-for-profit organizations."

"The Guthrie Center" is the name of the church building itself and the "interfaith spiritual center" housed within it. The Guthrie Foundation is a separate organization that runs most of the programs associated with the building. The two organizations were created separately so that potential donors who were unsure about the religious aspects of the center would not feel uncomfortable about supporting the foundation's programs.

In 1998 Guthrie Foundation manager Suzanne Florence gave a concrete example of the "responsive" approach at work. "One of the things that Arlo is personally very interested in doing is helping people with AIDS. When I came, I talked to the Red Cross and the Berkshire AIDS Coalition and asked what we could do to help. It turns out they're doing a very good job. We didn't need to do anything they were already doing, so we asked what they needed, and we found a volunteer to do grant writing for underfunded programs."

In September 1990, Arlo updated the readers of his newsletter on the progress of his quest to buy the church, establish a nonprofit organization, and move his home-based record company out of his home.

The folksinger, because he is a folksinger, is not now, and may never be likely to purchase the property personally. Therefore, he has created an entity which has filed for a tax-exempt status with the IRS and the Commonwealth of Massachusetts. This entity is called The Guthrie Center.

We sincerely hope that The Guthrie Center will be able to provide many more services to the local and global community than we were able to provide under the present circumstances. If we've learned anything from the likes of Woody Guthrie, and Pete and Toshi Seeger, it's that groups of ordinary folks can do things impossible for individual folks to do.

Organizations of all kinds are in place around the world doing wonderful work. We would like to establish our center as a place where people from these organizations, as well as individuals interested in such things, will come and learn from each other about our different cultures, religions, medical practices, and most of all, share in our different traditions of music and art . . .

When Rising Son began, we began as a way of salvaging our record catalog from obscurity. We grew when we were able to make available to you books, videos and recordings from Woody Guthrie, Pete Seeger and the Weavers. And there's a lot more coming. Our goal has been to inherit the past, preserve the present and hand down the future. And do it all gracefully.

If you have ever thought that you would like to help us, we could use that help now. Your contributions will be tax deductible as soon as we receive our tax-exempt status. If we are not able, for any reason, to acquire a tax-exempt status, we will send your contribution right back to you. We won't spend a dime of your donation on anything but the purchase of the building, unless we win the lottery or we raise more than the $320,000.00 we need.

There are about 4,500 subscribers to the RBR at present. There are 70,000 folks who just like getting postcards now and then. We also send a catalogue to everyone at least once a year. And this is that time. In other words, everyone we know is reading this. If every one of you 70,000 folks could manage to send us $5, we would have (the editor gets out his calculator) $350,000 and we would be able to pull this thing off.

Not surprisingly, Arlo takes a nontraditional approach to fund-raising. Although numerous experts told him to go after a few big donations instead of a greater number of smaller ones, Arlo decided to take the more difficult path. The response was not as great as he had hoped. Of all the people on the mailing list, about four hundred sent in donations. Eventually that total increased to four thousand. But little by little, he says, more people are supporting the organization and the build-ing by sending in $25 checks, and he sends a personal thank-you note to everyone who does.

"When I heard about that, I thought it was crazy, but nice," says Suzanne Florence, who signed on at the Guthrie Center in 1997. "This is how I think: 'You mean you send a personal thank-you note to everyone who sends a twenty-dollar check? You've got the cost of the paper, the stamp . . .' That's totally impractical, but it's nice and that's Arlo."

The first time he sent out the notes he discovered that it had an unexpected effect, as he recounted in his newsletter:

Famous folksinger Arlo Guthrie went crazy recently. He had discovered that many people had sent donations to his fledgling Guthrie Center and yet most, if not all, had gone unthanked. He went about scribbling Thank You Notes to everyone. Thank You Notes went pouring out of the old church by the letter load. All was well until he began receiv-ing notes, cards and letters thanking him for sending the Thank You Notes. He began to wonder if the Thank You Note program was such a good idea after all. A typical second generation Thank You Note went something like this: "I can't believe you sent me a Thank You Note in your actual own handwritten scribble . . . We couldn't make out the words but it was nice to get it anyway. Thanks so much. It made my minute!" Would he now have to write a Thank You for the Thank You Note reply? Sometimes it just boggles the mind. On behalf of The Guthrie Center and The Guthrie Foundation (a not-for-profit educational foundation), we wish to express our heartfelt thanks to everyone who made the effort to help us out of our financial difficulties. It is making a big difference around here. If there were some folks who made contributions and went unthanked, please contact the Thank You Note department immediately and you will receive your actual own handwritten scribble Thank You Note as soon as possible.

As of 1999, Arlo says, the Guthrie Center has between fifteen hundred and two thousand members who send in $25 a year. "Eventually we'll reach critical mass. When we get to that point, when I don't have to stay on the road another two months to cover that part of it, that allows me to do other things. Part of the other things I want to do is spend some time there. I know what has to happen there to make it feel welcoming and ennobling and all those good things. It's just the matter of getting the time and finding the staff."

When he'd come up with a financial plan, such as it was, there were still a few hurdles before he could take possession of the property. Once again, zoning was an issue. About twenty people showed up at a public hearing, held close to Thanksgiving in 1991, to see Arlo and hear his lawyer, Harris N. Aaronson, address the board, and a week later before the town selectmen. Arlo would need a variance because the building was on a half-acre lot in a one-acre residential zone and sat too close to the front and side property lines. In addition, he would need permission from the town's selectmen to move his office from his home to the church, which was in a residential zone. According to regulations, the Great Barrington selectmen could allow "professional offices" in a residential zone. So one of the questions they had to answer was whether he qualified as a "professional."

Even more important, however, was the question of whether or not

ED HYMAN, AUTOPHOTOS

Does this man look like a professional?

the neighbors wanted him there. Many of them had recent memories of that most famous period in the church's history — when Ray Brock's Trinity Racing Association drove motorcycles on the lawn and right through the door — memories that had been amplified and reinforced by the movie *Alice's Restaurant.* Outwardly, Arlo had not changed much since those days. The bearded forty-three-year-old's trademark mane of long curls had gone gray but still flowed well past his shoulders. He arrived at the hearing wearing jeans, rudraksha beads, and a windbreaker. He was one of the nation's most famous former flower children. So the neighbors wanted to know: Would he paint the church psychedelic colors and hold rock concerts there?

Zoning board member George T. Beebe asked the musician directly, "No motorcycles in and out the front door?"

Arlo did not remember any motorcycles inside the church. "We gotta remember that the movie was a movie," he said. "I never had a bike there." (In fact, Arlo never even rode a motorcycle in the film.)

For the most part, Arlo let the lawyer do the talking. "This is a once-in-a-lifetime opportunity to bring back together all those elements in the mystique of Alice's Church," he said. "We don't want to lose the heritage that started off in the stormy District Court in Lee."

The board granted the variance on the conditions that no parking be allowed on the front lawn and no structural changes be made to the exterior of the building without the board's permission.

A week later the selectmen ruled that Arlo was a professional, clearing the way, once he could afford it, to buy the church. The selectmen put their own conditions on the permit to operate a business. The first condition, curiously enough for a building that had been used as a private home for decades, was that no one could live in it. Other conditions were that no more than fifteen people could work there and it could not be the scene of activities that would result in a gathering.

There is a common misconception that the town was dead set against Arlo's owning the church and that they fought against his occupying it. In fact, this is far from the truth. Many previous tenants had tried to get permission to operate businesses of various kinds in the building, but were turned down. Arlo's proposal was accepted relatively quickly because the majority of the locals were pleased to see him back in the church. The Berkshire region of western Massachusetts is an area that treasures its history, whether in the form of colonial churches, historic inns, or a famous pop culture landmark of the 1960s. Having Arlo there would preserve that piece of local heritage. Arlo's suggestion that he would house a Woody Guthrie museum or archives in the church added to the historic and cultural appeal.

"The Guthrie mystique is very strong through Woody," Roland Ginzel says. "There's a generation who wanted him there because of Woody." His wife adds, "The community is very strong and very supportive, and I think they're proud to have him. They say, 'I knew Arlo when.'"

It was a lot of work turning the church into both an interfaith spiritual center and a record company office. New lighting had to be installed and a railing built for the stairs. Family and staff put desks and chairs into a van that Arlo's band had been using and into their own cars and brought them over to the church.

Arlo's return to the church was a great story. It was picked up by local, national, and international news; the *New York Times* ran a feature, as did a number of television stations. As Arlo and friends were moving furniture into the building, a crew from *Entertainment Tonight* was there filming.

"I thought, here's half a ton of garbage coming back in," Arlo told a *Berkshire Eagle* reporter. "It took twenty-five years to come full circle."

Arlo and Ma.

CRAIG F. WALKER, BERKSHIRE EAGLE

"It's a 'bring your own God' church."

— Arlo Guthrie

Housatonic, January 1992

B eing back at the church was cause for celebration. Despite the zoning regulation that allowed no more than fifteen people in the building at one time, Arlo told Sharon Palma to "invite everybody." The fact that more than fifteen people were going to show up could not have been a secret to anyone. The staff of Arlo's office got a list of local businesses from the Chamber of Commerce and sent invitations to all of them. They also sent invitations to all the neighbors and to everyone on Arlo's mailing list; they even addressed an invitation to "Town Hall." According to Sharon, the selectmen gave their verbal approval for the event. And even though they'd mailed out about 4,500 invitations, many of them were to people who lived so far away they weren't expected to come.

The celebration was to be more than just a party. It was going to be a rededication and reconsecration. As the press release for the event explained:

> On January 30th, Arlo Guthrie is hosting a rededication
> and a return to God of the former Trinity Church in Great

Barrington, Massachusetts, which he made famous in his landmark song Alice's Restaurant. Guthrie and his friends are celebrating the initial acquisition of the church as the new home for the Guthrie Foundation, a nonprofit organization which contributes to such causes as AIDS research, hospice and environmental protection. Arlo is inviting everyone he knows or knows of to come to the church and he's hoping many will contribute to the purchase of the building . . .

Speaking about the church, Guthrie said, "For a large group of us, the church symbolizes the same spirit that was at the heart of the controversies of the '60s — such as civil rights, the peace movement and the women's movement. Now, in addition to those on-going struggles, there are other concerns, like how to care for those suffering and living with AIDS and how we restore our environment." He added, "We want this church to be a center for service and sharing."

A number of prominent people are sitting on the Board of Trustees of the Guthrie Foundation, including Ram Dass, lecturer and former Harvard professor, and Toshi Seeger, organizer of the Hudson River Folk Festival and wife of Pete Seeger. Arlo is setting aside a portion of the church as a spiritual area, where people can pray, meditate, or simply sit in peace. He's calling it Ma's Hanuman Gar, dedicated both to his spiritual teacher, Ma Jaya Bhagavati, as well as to Hanuman, the God of service of Hinduism. Arlo said that much of his awareness and sensitivity to people who are suffering comes from Ma, who's very involved in working with hospice, abused children and with children and adults with AIDS. Every few months, Arlo travels to Florida and California and joins Ma on her rounds of hospices, AIDS clinics, and county homes. Ma, who will be assisting at the rededication ceremony, is also an artist with a growing national and international reputation, and a number of her paintings will be displayed for sale at the church, both to help the Foundation as well as her own service work.

Those who knew Arlo could not help but be aware of the significant role Ma played in his life, but until the grand opening of the Guthrie Center, the public was largely unaware of it. Although Arlo had been exploring his spirituality most of his life, it wasn't something he shared with reporters on a regular basis. Not that it was any secret; it was simply not something that often came up in conversation. It was part of his personal life, not his public life.

Arlo was born to a Jewish mother and a Protestant father. On that occasion, the nurse at the hospital asked Woody what religion to fill out for the child on the form. Woody said, "All." When the nurse said she couldn't write "All" on the form, he said to put "None." Not liking that answer, she went to Marjorie and asked her what religion the child was. Without consulting Woody, she also said, "All." The nurse again explained that she couldn't do that, so Marjorie, too, said, "Then put 'None.'"

"Woody was very religious about life," Marjorie once said. "He knew the Bible chapter and verse. And after we got married — I'm Jewish — he read the Talmud, but he never talked religion to the children. He used to say to them all religions were the same. He felt everything very keenly but he didn't talk much. Arlo's the same way."

At thirteen, Arlo celebrated what has been called "possibly the world's first hootenany bar mitzvah." While he never left his Jewish roots entirely behind, as a young adult he became interested in Eastern and New Age thought. He told Arsenio Orteza of *Christian Century* magazine, "I always liked that Jesus character too. I didn't know if he was God or what, but I liked him. He was like a hero. But there were others. Lao-Tzu was a hero of mine, and maybe a few other philosophers and theologians here and there — nobody who I thought would end up as the be-all and end-all of my life, but people who intrigued me. I was also interested in Eastern mysticism, old Christian mysticism, and Jewish mysticism."

During the success of *Alice's Restaurant*, Arlo became a vegetarian and was widely reported to be a serious student of astrology. His mother told a reporter she thought being a vegetarian was OK, as long as Arlo was healthy, and that she hoped he would "outgrow his occult phase."

One of his favorite songs to play at the church, back when it was owned by Alice and Ray, was "Amazing Grace." Even in some of his earliest concerts he closed with the song and asked the audience to sing along. He often described music in spiritual terms.

"The object of music has to be as an equalizer of yin and yang things that produce a feeling of balance and harmony in the audience," he once said. "It could take a hundred years to do it right."

A number of factors probably helped fuel his interest in religious studies. Interviews he did when he was only twenty-two suggest that he suspected he had inherited Huntington's chorea, the disease that had slowly killed his father, and that he would himself die young.

"You know what I've got, don't you?" he said. "I've got to pile a complete lifetime into maybe a few more years. I don't know how many, really. That's the bad part of it all . . . It's a funny thing to walk around just feeling fine and knowing that the big fellow in black may slide up to you any day and say, 'What's with you, Arlo boy? Don't you know there's not much time? We got an appointment'. . . In a way I'm lucky. Not too many people know how they're going to die. It takes a lot of the pressure and worry off you about your future. Of course, I ain't in no hurry to get there — but then I don't worry about being hit by a car on the street anymore."

He would later say that he didn't remember ever being overly concerned about getting the disease. When a test was developed in the 1970s that could determine if he carried the gene for Huntington's chorea, Arlo decided against taking it.

"So what if I have it? Am I going to do something different with my life?" he wrote in *People* magazine. "If you're going to do something different because you've found out you've got a disease, then you're not living as you should be . . . You can enjoy being alive for however long you're alive. You shouldn't ever have to look over your shoulder and say, 'I should have done something else.'"

Whether or not he thought he had inherited Huntington's chorea, his father's condition had Arlo considering his own mortality at an age when most people feel immortal. Meanwhile, as a famous person, one who was dubbed the "spokesman of his generation," other people looked to him for answers. *Esquire* printed a drawing of countercultural figures seated as in the painting *The Last Supper,* under the heading "Last Supper at Alice's Restaurant." "Picture your old man sitting at home wondering who you do trust," the accompanying article began. "Not him, and certainly not your college president. Cut out this painting and send it to him. These, for his information, are twenty-eight people he might not listen to, but you would — if they were around to tell you anything." The first character in the painting was Arlo.

Look magazine recorded an incident when a fan came up to Arlo and asked, "When did you know you were going to be doing what you're doing?" Arlo replied, "Oh, about three-four years ago." The fan said, "Yeah! Hey! It's like with Christ! Just like Christ! He knew he would be the Messiah!" Arlo was startled and said firmly, "No, man, I'm no Messiah," and walked away, looking down and seemingly shaken.

So Arlo was driven both internally and externally to seek answers, and motivated as well by other forces only he can fully understand. Then, in the 1970s, he had a mystical experience, as he recounted to Arsenio Orteza: "I was standing on my porch and one of those things happened that I never imagined would happen to me. I don't know how to explain it, and I don't want to make a big deal out of it, but God showed up in the person of Jesus Christ. He was sort of right in front of me. I knew who he was even though nobody said anything. And not only that, but I knew that he knew everything about me. For about ten minutes — actually I have no idea how long it was — I felt a love that I knew existed but that I never thought I would be in the midst of. And it penetrated every atom of my being."

The episode drew out his latent spirituality. He went to "the first church I came to," a Catholic church, and began studying. He befriended some Catholic brothers and eventually became a third-order Franciscan.

Around this time he told author Joe Klein, "This whole thing has been as surprising to me as it must be to you. What do you think of when you think of the Catholic Church? You think of oppression, right? But you got to get beyond that. See, I've been through all the other things, all the gurus and things you pick up one week because TV is boring or your old lady is pissed, and then you drop them. But this is different. This is the real thing. And you got to remember that in the beginning I was as skeptical as you."

Later, however, he *would* find a guru whom he would not pick up and drop so quickly. He learned about her during a difficult period in his life, not long after Warner Brothers had rejected "Someday." Of this time, Arlo told Orteza, "My marriage was sometimes on the rocks, the kids were sometimes going nuts, and sometimes the work was too hard or just too crazy."

In 1982, the same year that Warner Brothers cut him loose, Arlo learned that his mother had cancer. Although much has been made of Woody Guthrie's role in shaping Arlo's personality, Arlo has often said that he was more influenced by having a professional mother than a "legendary" father.

Marjorie Guthrie had always been full of life and active for social causes. During Woody's illness and after his death she became a tireless campaigner for Huntington's chorea research. She single-handedly founded the Committee to Combat Huntington's Disease. She was also largely responsible for preserving and promoting Woody's work as well as the work of her mother, poet Aliza Greenblatt.

She was a highly active member of a number of organizations, including the National Yiddish Book Center. Aaron Lansky, another member, says that one of his favorite memories involving Marjorie was of a 1981 reception she had hosted to gain support for the organization. Stage actor and musician Theodore Bikel "took down a guitar from the wall — a half-size model, the first guitar Woody had given to Arlo — and began to play Yiddish folk songs written by Aliza Greenblatt. Such a meeting of two worlds only Marjorie Guthrie could inspire."

Marjorie Guthrie passed away on the morning of March 13, 1983. She was sixty-five. A month later a memorial service was held in New York. Hundreds of people came to pay tribute to a woman who had touched so many people's lives. Among those in attendance were Helen Hayes, Pete Seeger, Pearl Lang, Sophie Maslow, Joe Klein, and numerous physicians, scientists, and congressmen.

Out of these trying times the next phase of Arlo's spiritual journey was born. In the summer of 1985, he recorded a pivotal event in the *Rolling Blunder Review*:

> I saw her picture at Laura's house on the Vineyard. Laura had lived with us at our house in the Berkshires and had been an old and dear friend. "Who's that?" I asked, looking at the photograph.
>
> "That's Ma," she said.
>
> "I want to meet her," I said.
>
> "You can't just meet her. She's a holy woman and she lives in Florida on an ashram with lots of yogis. You have to call way in advance and see if you can make an appointment."

"So. Call her up," I said.

"You mean right now?" Laura looked at me like I was losing it.

"Yeah."

Laura called the office at the ashram later that evening and someone informed her that they would be back in touch with us sometime soon. The next morning Laura had this message: "Tell him he can come, but he comes at his own risk."

"Hey, Laura, what do you think that means, 'comes at his own risk'? Huh?" I asked.

"I don't know." She shrugged. "It's just what they said to tell you."

Within a few days I was heading to Florida — just on a whim. I went to the airport and stood before an old airplane. It was the kind where you enter through the rear and walk uphill through the cabin. It looked like a cartoon plane.

The stewardess held the mic up to her mouth. "Welcome aboard the airplane with the most flying time ever recorded by a commercial airliner. This plane has flown for . . ." She continued to tell the passengers the story.

I was getting ready to go to heaven. No wonder they warned me. I was coming at my own risk, all right! I was about to die. But, I got to Florida safely. I met Jaya Sati Bhagavati Ma, or Ma. And nothing could have prepared me for Ma, and only Ma could have prepared me for the next decade. I was about to die all right, but not in the usual sense . . . The journey I had been waiting for had finally begun.

Although Ma teaches service primarily through the Hindu path of yoga, her main philosophy is to incorporate all that is holy from every religious tradition. This approach intuitively appealed to Arlo, who has merged his Jewish background, Catholic training, and Hindu studies into his own, highly individual approach to life.

"There's no battle going on inside me between the Jewish part of my life, the Christian part, or for that matter the Buddhist and the Hindu," he told a *Berkshire Eagle* reporter. "They all live very happily within me. That's how I know they can live happily outside me."

Ma became Arlo's teacher and spiritual role model — in his words, his "wonderful guru." In 1999, in response to fans who questioned the wisdom of having a guru, Arlo posted this explanation on the Internet newsgroup alt.music.guthrie:

> God does not have to find you. He already knows where you are. He may invite you but the decision to find the truth within your own heart is yours alone and is a difficult journey at times. That's why all serious religions require that priests, ministers, rabbis, etc. — study with those who have made the journey. Being wise is not always easy. There were pitfalls along the way even for Solomon. In India, a guru is someone who has made the journey. Are there fakes and frauds? Sure. Anyone can repeat religious truths from books they've read or from other people. Personally, I would not want as a guide someone who has never been there. There is no question at all in my mind that "God is love and that those who live in love, live in God and He in them" to quote Neem Karoli Baba. I am sure that all true lovers of the truth go to the truth, whatever they may call it, whether they are Buddhist, Hindu, Jew, Christian or whatever . . . How do I know these things? Jesus came to me 20 something years ago on my front porch. He came to a nice Jewish kid! His love started me on the journey of this lifetime and I have been at his feet ever since. He brought me to my Guru who loves like no other and I have been at her feet ever since. I bow before every human who has endured the journey of death to the self and life to God. I treat with reverence all I meet on the road of the cross — those who die so they may live. Whatever they call themselves, I call them friends and teachers. Thank God for God! Jai Kalima!

Shortly after Arlo met his guru, he learned that his interest in Eastern religion was another thing he had in common with his father. As he told author Joanna Powell, the subject came up during a conversation with Woody's first wife, Mary, with whom Arlo had maintained a friendship.

"I told her a little about what I was into," he said. "That I had started doing meditation and yoga and that I was really happy. That it had changed my life to some extent and that I thought it was making me a better human being. I had found my teacher, my guru, those kinds of things. I didn't want to say too much because I thought, This is a Texas girl who probably doesn't know too much about this, let alone have an interest. She nearly floored me when she said, 'Oh, that's interesting. Your father used to do all of that too.' 'You're kidding!' I said. When he was young and she was dating him in Pampa, Texas, he used to take courses and study meditation and read books on Eastern philosophy. She described some of the things he did, and I instantly recognized that we shared something much deeper than I had ever imagined. I went home and started going through some of his things, some of his books that ended up with me. Sure enough, I found books on Eastern philosophy, yoga, meditation, books about work on one's personal self that he had studied. He had written into the margins. He was a great underliner and a big note taker and I thought that it was so wonderful to share his thoughts some fifty years later. Because it wasn't of any interest to his friends or companions, none of them ever told me anything about it."

The Guthrie Center, which was named for Woody, not Arlo, would reflect the values of both father and son as inspired by Arlo's guru. "I saw it as a way to preserve the values that other people found important," Arlo explains. "The values that I have I didn't just invent. They came from my dad and from my mom and from my teachers and people I had known. That's why I named the center after my dad. I thought that some of his philosophy was worth talking about. And I thought it would be nice to have a place where those kinds of ideas are respected, not just a museum where people go to find out about it but a place where people are actually doing something."

The sanctuary itself would be known as "Ma's Hanuman Ghar," which translates to "Ma's House of Hanuman." ("Ma's Hanuman Gar," which appeared in the press release and, for some time, on a carved wooden sign over the side door of the sanctuary, was a misspelling. Asked if the center would be putting the sign back up soon, Arlo replied, "Not with that spelling.")

"Hanuman" is Arlo's spiritual name, given to him by his guru. Hanuman is the Hindu monkey god of service. The temple of Neem Karoli Baba, Ma's own guru, was named for the god. (Neem Karoli Baba was also the guru of former Harvard professor Richard Alpert, whose spiritual name, Ram Dass, was given to him by the teacher and also means "Hanuman.")

In the sacred epic poem *Ramayana*, Hanuman is a servant of Rama, a compassionate god who comes to Earth to rid the universe of demons (*rakshashas*) led by a demon king, Ravana. Hanuman, chief of the monkeys, comes to Rama's aid in a great

Ma's Hanuman Ghar, here decorated for a Thanksgiving dinner. The plaque to the right near the organ is dedicated to John Coffing.

battle for the rescue of his wife, Sita. As a result of his single-minded devotion to his master, Hanuman is blessed with great powers. He is able to leap across the ocean and find Sita. This is but the first of a number of extraordinary feats he performs. He is revered by Hindus throughout India, and his birth anniversary, Hanuman Jayanti, is observed with fasting and celibacy and the reading of a special prayer, the Hanuman-Chalisa. Hindus go to the many temples in his honor to offer prayers and repaint his image with vermilion. For his unselfish devotion to Rama, Hanuman is known as "the embodiment of selfless service." He is a symbol of heroism and valor in the battle for truth, devotion, service, and humility.

The son of the wind god Vaayu, Hanuman is thus also known as the "son of the wind," a title Arlo used for an album of cowboy songs. Hanuman's presence is evident throughout the church on banners and drawings as well as on the destination marker on Arlo's tour bus.

The trinitarian symbolism of the church architecture itself could equally apply to the three gods of the Hindu trinity, Shiva, Vishnu, and Brahma. In Christian tradition, the arched apse and the cruciform shape of the sanctuary represent the destruction and renewal of Noah's Ark, from Jewish tradition, and Christ's passion, from Christianity. The gods of the Hindu trinity likewise represent the cycle of destruction and renewal. Brahma is the creator, Vishnu the preserver, and Shiva the destroyer. The triad makes up the supreme formless being (Brahm) that rules the cosmos.

With the ceremony dedicating the center, Arlo would once again address the question that Venable Herndon had posed in the movie *Alice's Restaurant*: "When society deconsecrates a church, can a new society reconsecrate it?" This time, Arlo hoped the answer would be yes.

"I have a feeling that Ma thought this was something he needed to do," Sharon Palma says. "So she probably encouraged the whole thing."

Because Ma, not to mention everyone else Arlo knew, was going to be at the dedication, it was important that everything be perfect. Volunteers helped with cleaning, planting flowers, and getting the newsletters out. To prepare for the opening night, Arlo and his staff put down red carpeting and turned the former altar back into an altar. On it they placed symbols of the world's religions: rosary beads, a menorah, statues of Hindu gods, and a crucifix, along with candles, incense, and pictures of Ma and Neem Karoli Baba. On the wall they hung Ma's poem, which sums up her outlook and is also the underlying philosophy of the Guthrie Center:

> One God, many forms
> One River, many streams
> One people, many faces
> One Mother, many children.

"Arlo's got this grand idea in his head about the building, and it's good," Rick Robbins says. "It's the Guthrie Center and it stands for a lot of the things that Woody stood for — being open." Recalling the anecdote about the hospital forms, he adds, "Take the good out of 'all' and put it in one place and use it. That's what the church is. It's whatever you want it to be. It doesn't matter what religion you are. You can do whatever you want, creatively. I think that's Arlo's vision. And to preserve the Woody Guthrie legacy. Woody had this ability to remain a child. That's why a lot of people loved him. A lot of people hated him, too, because he never grew up. And in some ways Arlo's a lot like Woody. He's got the ability to be a kid. And he's got a great sense of humor."

The Guthrie Center is "reconsecrated."

The opening night was by all accounts a crazy event. Alice and Officer Obie were there, along with hundreds of friends, fans, and neighbors. It resembled the Thanksgiving scene in *Alice's Restaurant,* in which people of all descriptions arrive at the church from every part of the country, by plane, train, and automobile, except that it was more crowded. Arlo did not realize Bill Obanhein had come until he walked up on stage.

Cars were parked on all the neighbors' lawns, blocking traffic on Van Deusenville Road. People who arrived late had to be turned away. There was no place to put them. There was plenty of food — spaghetti, bread, coffee, cookies, and covered dishes. A school bus driver who lived near the church arrived with a foil-covered plate of sweets.

"The opening night with Ma was a stunning evening," Arlo says. "Mostly because we had so many people there. All the engineers and the construction guys were standing on the sides because the floor was bowed and they thought it was going to break. All the idiots like me were sitting in the middle. The floor was actually bowed about a foot and a half.

We've never had that many people in there before or after. Luckily the floors were supported by structures underneath. They put them there when they did the movie so they could move the cameras on the big dollies without the floor moving. So they had secured some of the church."

The ceremony lasted about an hour and a half. Alice was brought to center stage and somewhat self-consciously received enthusiastic applause. Two Franciscan brothers from Villanova University gave their blessings. And then there was Ma.

"My wonderful guru came in, and we reconsecrated the church because it had been deconsecrated," Arlo says. "We thought it would be fun to reconsecrate it, that is, return it to the service for which it had been built in the first place. Simply, dedication to God and service to mankind, that's what churches are, all of them, whether they're synagogues, mosques, temples. Everything glorifies and everything serves."

PETIE BOGEN-GARRETT

Arlo and Ma meet the press.

Ma was described by the *Berkshire Record*'s reporter as "a spiritual Ethel Merman wielding a Brooklyn persona" and a "fiftyish in-your-face guru." Ma sported long dark hair that framed a face adorned with a *tilaka* (a mark worn on the forehead as a symbol of religious affiliation). She was dressed in a shimmering black and gold tunic and gilded chains. She shouted to be heard by the assembled multitude, but her voice was clear and strong. She told the audience to make believe it was the 1960s and to love each other. "The door is open to all. Come and work with us," she said. She introduced Gary, a man from Albany who had AIDS, kissed him, and had her young son kiss him as well. Many of the people there found it to be a deeply moving, spiritual experience.

"I don't think you could have fit two more people in there," says Sherry Boullt, a longtime Arlo supporter. "I remember sitting there imagining living in this building. This movie that I'd watched and this song that I'd heard were so much more real. I don't know what I was expecting [from Ma], but I didn't expect an accent that was so familiar, it's like having a Jewish grandmother looking over your shoulder. You walked away realizing that you were family, everyone who was there, whether you knew them or not. We knew that whatever was going to happen there was going to be special."

Of course, not everyone had the same reaction to the event and to Ma. "She was this absolutely exotic woman," says one observer. "There was a couch and a couple of people who obviously weren't well, and she started to do a promotion of her thing. She totally upstaged Arlo and Alice. Every once in a while she'd snap her fingers and say, 'Let's have a song, Arlo.'"

Alice says the whole thing made her uncomfortable. "I didn't like Ma. This was Arlo's guru. I didn't want to make a big stink, but this woman was like a queen. I went. I was happy for Arlo. He wanted me there, so I went. I thought it was kind of ludicrous. Once she was being filmed and she pushed me out of the way. I was just kind of laughing. Here is this dame, she's my age, she's from Brooklyn, she's Jewish, just like me, but she had this giant scam. You become a leader, you become a religious figure, and people worship you, and they pay."

Former Trinity Church member Mary Sachs came to the event and found it overwhelming. "[Arlo] took me to the opening. He came down with this woman with all the beads and he said, 'This is Ma.' And I said, 'She's your mother?' Can you imagine? I didn't know. Then they went up on the altar. He had Obanhein, and he had someone with AIDS, and they wanted me to go up there and I refused. And he was going to play, and all the people had to sit on the floor, and that's when I left."

Before the evening was over, the seeds had been planted for a new set of rumors. Arlo Guthrie had gone crazy, he was bringing in a flamboyant guru and people with AIDS, and he was going to start a new religious cult in the Berkshires. They were going to use their nonprofit, religious organization status to get around bylaws and open a restaurant. There would probably be drugs, littering, and motorcycles involved in some way. There goes the neighborhood.

"A lot of neighbors went, 'Whoa! There are people with AIDS here,'" Arlo remembers. "And Ma started talking about abused children and people said, 'Whoa! There are probably abused people around here. Maybe sitting next to me.' And a lot of people got uncomfortable even though we'd invited the neighbors, we'd invited all these people, and said, 'Isn't this great.' People walked away thinking, 'We don't know if this is great or not.' And we created a division."

What Sharon Palma remembers about the event was mostly its aftermath. "Especially since Arlo and crew just left two days afterwards [for an eight-week tour], and I had to sit there and talk to people. That's when I learned to speak to the press very quickly. A couple of neighbors really got their noses out of joint. First of all it was Arlo, and he was this long-haired hippie, and they had visions of motorcycles going into the church and the fact that he had a guru kind of scared the hell out of some people. They kind of overreacted."

A few of the neighbors went to the town selectmen and asked them to revoke his permit to operate a business in the church.

"This is a very small neighborhood," one neighbor said. "The neighborhood would be up in arms if we knew he was going to bring in homeless children and people with AIDS. There's got to be a guru bylaw that puts this thing into nonconforming and starts them all over again."

"He bamboozled the neighborhood, and he bamboozled the town," said another. "He thinks because he's somebody he can do whatever he wants."

To complicate matters, Arlo soon thereafter announced plans to conduct a seminar on holistic healing as one of the first events at the Guthrie Center. The neighbors, who were already concerned about what he was doing there, grew even more wary and took the matter to the selectmen. Because the Guthrie Center was registered as a religious institution, they could not deal with it in the same way they would deal with a business. One of the selectmen told the *Eagle* that Arlo had found a "loophole" in the law. On the road in California, Arlo replied, "The First Amendment is not a loophole." That statement was later adopted by the Institute for First Amendment Studies as the quote of the year.

"That's one of the quotes that I love," Arlo says. "The things that I wanted to do there and the way that we wanted to do them are very important in preserving the liberties of a lot of other people. Unlike guys like Larry Flynt, or guys who use the First Amendment for their own purposes and their own financial gain, there's nothing in this for me personally. There's no salary I get from having the church that I wasn't making before I had the church. So what we're trying to do there has been misunderstood by people who thought that I had found some way around various laws and ordinances."

As a public figure in a relatively quiet region, anything Arlo did was likely to make headlines. In fact, the local newspaper once ran a blurb saying that "Arlo Guthrie has run afoul of the law again." He had received a parking ticket.

If buying the church was a good story, then wrangling with the neighbors over buying the church — complete with a colorful guru and parallels to *Alice's Restaurant* — was a great story. The local newspaper, the *Berkshire Eagle*, covered it, of course. Because it involved a celebrity, it landed on the front page. Other papers in the region also covered the story. It was on page A1 of the *Times Union* in Albany, New York. The *New York Times* ran a story that was eventually picked up by the Associated Press.

Sharon Palma fielded the calls and responded to the rumors. No, Arlo and his wife were not breaking up; Arlo had camped out at the church a couple of nights because he wanted to spend more time at the place. No, Arlo was not starting a new religion. No, Ma was not moving to the Berkshires. No, they did not plan to deceive the neighbors about anything they were doing. Yes, they had brought in more than fifteen people but they hadn't known they needed to ask the Board of Health about it. "We didn't understand we had to ask for every little thing or we would have done it," Sharon told the *Berkshire Eagle*. "We're trying to help people. We're not trying to ruin the neighborhood. I hope someday they'll forget about it all."

Behind the scenes, Arlo made plans to talk with the selectmen about their concerns when he came back from his tour. As the *Times Union* reported, "For most of Great Barrington, the dispute out on Van Deusenville Road seems pretty unimportant."

That didn't stop the story from taking on a life of its own in the press. Letters, calls, and faxes came into Great Barrington from as far away as Germany — so many, in fact, that other town business had to be put on hold for three days.

"The truth is that most of the people there are decent people," Arlo says. "And for the next three years there were articles in the paper all written by the same journalist, all referring to the same four people, all of whom had the same three things to say. One who misunderstood what was going on there eventually came by and said, 'I'm sorry I said the things I said. This is all ridiculous. I didn't mean it.' They didn't retract anything. They wouldn't let it go. It sold newspapers."

News clippings from the *Berkshire Eagle* reveal this "three years" to be something of an exaggeration. Articles on the grand opening of the Guthrie Center and the subsequent disputes with the neighbors ran in the local paper for several months before the press and the public lost interest, although other publications undoubtedly followed up on the story much later. After several stories on Arlo and his intentions for the center, the folksinger decided to buy a page in the *Berkshire Eagle* to present his side of the story. It read:

To the Editor of The Eagle:
It is time to put an end to the constant barrage of misinformation that has been flooding the press locally and internationally. Friend and foe alike have been misrepresented which, frankly, hurts the image of the town of Great Barrington more than my critics or myself. The public has been led to believe that the town of Great Barrington wants to revoke our permits and kick us out of Alice's Church. I want my friends to know that this is just not true. So far, the town has been tremendously supportive. The Selectmen have asked to meet with me to clarify what we are doing, and we are eagerly awaiting the chance to do just that. Meanwhile, there is no justification for anyone to become angry or indignant with anyone, over the phone or through the mail, over the alleged controversy. Neighbors and local officials want to be assured that we were not being deceptive when we applied for our permits, and that we are abiding by the conditions

we agreed to. We have already, I hope, assured the Selectmen that we are not in violation of any condition. And I am quite confident that I will be able to remove any doubts concerning the alleged bamboozling, back-stabbing, sneaky, underhanded, guru-crazed, bead-wearing, motorcycling way that we run our charities.

Arlo says he was never really bothered by the controversy. For the most part he found it amusing. In the midst of it he told local music reporter Seth Rogovoy, "I'm beginning to get that old, familiar feeling when you know that you are in the middle of something very funny and you can't quite tell what's funny about it." He said he was going to come out with a new tea called "Bamboozled." "There's a picture of the church on the cover with people running out the doors and screaming like in a monster movie. It's a high-energy tea."

The controversy had a number of effects on operations at the

Arlo plants a tree in his new yard.

Guthrie Center. On the one hand, the staff was cautious about sponsoring too many activities that would further exacerbate the conflict with the neighbors. On the other hand, the controversy brought a great deal of attention to the fledgling nonprofit organization. Many of the people who sent messages to the town offices in Great Barrington also sent their support to the center.

One of those to visit the church after reading about it in the newspaper was a local preacher. As Arlo recalls, "I was mopping up the floor, and the local preacher came by. He said, 'I just came by to see what you're doing here.' I said, 'I'm just mopping up.' He said, 'No, Arlo, what are you *doing* here?' I said, 'What do you mean?' He said, 'Arlo, what kind of church is this?' No one had ever asked me before. So I said, 'Well, it's a "bring your own God" church.' Just a spontaneous answer to a question." It is one of his favorite memories, and it has become an unofficial motto of the Guthrie Center.

Arlo Guthrie, Rick Robbins, and Paul Kleinwald play together at the Stockbridge School reunion held in 1998 at the Guthrie Center.

ED HYMAN, AUTOPHOTOS

"It's nice to have it back in the family," Rick Robbins says. "Because what it represented back then it can represent now — the idea of having the church and being able to go there and being able to do whatever you want. I think it was always in the back of our minds that there was a lot of spirituality there. It became a sort of church like it is now, bring your own God. But we never thought about that. We just knew it was a great building. I think Arlo, and myself and a lot of people who were part of that circle of friends, feel that it's nice. I feel that it's nice that I can go over and walk through the door. I can go when Arlo is there or he's not there. It's there for being creative."

It took a while for the furor to die down. There was the obligatory article commenting on Arlo's open letter and the reaction to the article reacting to the editorial, but eventually the story did run its course in the newspapers. The neighbors who had complained went on to other things, and there have been few, if any, conflicts since.

Arlo insists that he's really not a troublemaker. "Arlo Guthrie — trouble. It's like three words that went together. People who want to believe bad things about their neighbors because it suits them will continue to do that for long periods of time no matter what the truth is. People who were genuinely interested were generally the minority of people. It's like in any small town. You might have some people who are for something, some people who are against it — that's probably four percent of the whole population. The rest of the ninety-six percent doesn't care one way or the other. But the newspaper only quotes the four percent, and if they can find the ones who are the most negative, they're going to talk to them first. That's just the way that works. The only time I did something wrong around here was the time we took the garbage and put it in the wrong place. Not to forget that there was already garbage there. It's not like we started our own dump. I'm not making an excuse, but I'm saying the only thing we ever really did wrong and ran afoul of the law was putting the garbage in the wrong place. It wasn't a half a ton, either. That's my exaggeration. That doesn't mean I haven't had conflicts with local officials. It's taken a long time to get that stuff behind us and move on, although frankly it never bothered me personally. None of the troubles that I ever had were serious to begin with."

"The church . . . has opportunity for doing much good. May God finish the work he has begun."

— Reverend Samuel Parker
First rector of Trinity Church, 1840

Housatonic, 1992

When the offices of Rising Son Records were located in the church, the lobby of the Guthrie Center had an air of both soothing calm and hectic craziness. When the church had been used as a house, both the big wooden front doors had been removed and replaced with windows to let in more light. One of the first things Arlo did was to restore one of the doors, the one underneath the rose window, to its original condition. The result is that the front room, with its dark wood paneling and cozy fireplace, is dimly lit. It looks very much like the living room it used to be. The air is tinged with incense, and the sunny kitchen just off to the left magnifies the sense of being at home. But when Rising Son was still housed there, the phones rang often, breaking the spell, and the staff members were busy and often distracted, constantly counting and recounting in their heads all the things they had to take care of.

"It's a really relaxed atmosphere," says former Guthrie Foundation manager Suzanne Florence. "It's almost like working at home. There's something really nice about it. But my job isn't a relaxed job."

Far from it, especially in the early days, when the staff of the record company doubled as the staff on the nonprofit side. Suzanne came along later, when the jobs were separated. Sharon, who handled all three organizations, remembers the fast-paced job fondly. "The whole job was kind of stressful in a fun kind of way. There was so much going on and it was so busy, and I thrived on it. And this just added one more level to it."

Arlo admits that he was not "born to run a nonprofit." The opportunity had presented itself, and he had jumped in with no experience. It is not surprising, then, that it took a little time for the organization to find its direction. Since he took on the task, though, Arlo has learned a lot through trial and error.

Guthrie Center volunteers Sherry Boullt and Pam Ross.

There were a number of obvious obstacles from the start. First, there was the state of the building to contend with. Before the funding could find its way to programs, some of it would have to be invested in resolving the building's structural problems, many of which dated back to its days as a church. The sanctuary was still unheated, making it impossible to use for several months of the year. Other problems were newer. The facade was covered in brown peeling paint that had once been white, there were bees in the bell tower, and from time to time a mouse would crawl into a wall and die there, smelling up the rooms.

Before people went home for the day, they would cover up their

computers with garbage bags. "I thought they were just really dust con-
scious," Suzanne says, "but it turns out the roof was leaking and the rain
would fall down right on the equipment. The bell tower had water
coming in. People were running up with garbage pails."

Besides being a "bring your own God" church, it was, at least in one
case, a "bring your own desk" church. One of the volunteers spent so
much time at the center that they finally hired her as a secretary. The only
problem was, they didn't have a desk for her, so she brought one from home.
No one can remember whether she brought the desk because she had
the job or she got the job because she brought the desk.

Then there was the fact that Arlo spent about ten months of the year
on the road. Originally he tried to run everything long-distance with his
laptop and a telephone, but it became clear early on that there were major flaws in this plan.

Sherry Boullt, an early volunteer at the center, said everyone involved
was thrilled at the opportunity to do something positive but found it
hard to coordinate around a folksinger's schedule. "You want him to be
at this celebrity auction and it ends up being really difficult to put
together. Of course if he weren't on the road doing his thing, then people
might not be as interested. It would be awesome if there were two of him."

Eventually Arlo realized that he would need a full-time manager to
take care of the nonprofit organizations. The first person to hold that
position was Jimmy Griffis, who joined the staff in 1997 and secured
some of the first grant funding for the organizations. Even with a full-
time manager, however, Arlo was not ready to turn over complete
control of operations. As he puts it, "From a practical point of view there
has to be someone in control, so I end up being that. I like being the boss
of things anyway. Probably because I'm a firstborn type and I've run my
own show on the road for so long that I'm just used to it. So I enjoy that.
I enjoy directing the events that go on there and deciding what goes on
there and what ain't. I haven't always been smart about those things, but
the more I do it the smarter I get. I hope that it will provide all the people
that belong to it with some kind of shared experiences that let people
feel like they're doing something that feels worthwhile."

Although Suzanne says things were filed literally under P for "Prob-
ably/Probably Not" when she got there, a year after Jimmy's stay, she
says Arlo is quite serious about his work and far from the burned-out

hippie some people might imagine him to be.

Although he is a good businessman, he is also a dreamer and an idealist. Some of his most imaginative and ambitious plans are difficult to bring to fruition. The job of the Guthrie Center manager often is to take an idea that seems fanciful or unfeasible and figure out how to make it possible. At her first staff meeting, Suzanne thought Arlo was joking about some of his ideas. She quickly realized he was not.

"Arlo has all these ideas — these weird, creative ideas," she says. "Making them a reality is not always easy. He had this idea for the cyber center. I had to see if that was something we could even do. What organizations would we have to work with? What equipment would we need? Could we afford the technology? I had to get estimates on video conferencing and see what it would cost and can we do it. Sometimes they work. Sometimes they won't work. He is the kind of person you have to show things. You have to show him, look, this will not work, and here is why. You have to let him see it. I think it has a lot of potential to do a lot of great things. All the ingredients are there. It just needs someone to put the ingredients together. It just needs someone to give it a push."

This is not to say that nothing happened at the center in the early days, but these forces and the desire to avoid any further rifts with the neighbors did delay some of the more ambitious projects. Following Arlo's free-form vision of the place, the programs that were launched began through the initiatives of specific individuals who happened to have special skills or were aware of particular needs in the community. For example, the first program initiated by the center, an ongoing program, was musical visits for troubled youths. One of the musicians on Arlo's album "Son of the Wind" was Rick Tiven, who was also a teacher at the Hillcrest School, an institution for children aged six to fourteen who had been abused, neglected, or abandoned. He suggested a program that would allow the kids to come to the church and play music. While the furor over Arlo's plans for the center raged in the newspapers, the children came to the church for the first time, had breakfast with Arlo, and played harmonicas, guitars, and keyboards. Although more than half of the newspaper story covering the program was devoted to the continuing dispute with the neighbors and rumors about Arlo's activities, it also quoted a ten-year-old boy who said, "I never did anything like this before" and added that the chocolate chip cookies brought by volunteers tasted good.

Over time other programs were developed, based on the skills of the volunteers and the needs of the community. Eventually the mission of the foundation evolved into "a not-for-profit educational foundation . . . formed to help provide local cultures with the means to preserve its music, stories, medicine, dance and spiritual traditions in the face of an ever encroaching global identity."

In practical terms, this translates into art programs and cooking classes for kids and a children's music program run by musician David Grover. Other community organizations also use the space, for anything from Girl Scout training to blood pressure clinics, lecture series, or pre-natal yoga classes. In the future, the center plans to have Internet and video conferencing to allow children to communicate with their peers from other cultures around the world. Last but not least, the organization exists to restore the historic church and keep it available to those who would like to visit.

There have been a number of memorable events at the church since Arlo purchased it. In November 1992, he hosted a Thanksgiving fund-raising dinner with food prepared by Alice. The invitation was sent to about four hundred people, including three of the town's selectmen. It said, in part:

> Come and enjoy the frenzy your presence will create as our neighbors go nuts, the media goes berserk and I go to the dump once again.
>
> We are not a religion. We are a diverse collection of strange people from many different religious backgrounds who share in common the belief that the best way to solve your own problems is to help somebody who has more problems than you do.

Sharon Palma assured local reporters that the invitation was meant to be "cute," not controversial.

"The church is Thanksgiving and Arlo is Thanksgiving," says Sherry Boullt, who attended the fund-raising feast. "There we were having Thanksgiving in the church with Arlo. It was another of those moment-in-time kind of things."

Arlo hands sister Nora a sheet with her winning bid on Bob Dylan's jacket.

JUDY BEISLER

There was also a celebrity auction. Some of the items available to bidders were Norman Rockwell's shoes and Bob Dylan's jacket, which Arlo's sister Nora took with a winning bid. And of course there was the rerecording of "Alice's Restaurant," more than thirty years after the original events took place, in the building where they took place.

The rerecording of "Alice" happened for a number of reasons. Arlo has said that he wanted to rerecord the album the day it came out. The album was recorded quickly. As he put it, "As long as it takes to listen to it is how long it took to make it." On a scale of one to ten, he believes the recording was a 7.5 or 8. Some people who have heard tapes of the song as it was performed on WBAI say they wish that version had found its way onto an album. Arlo has often toyed with the idea of putting out a CD of some of the various prototype versions of his anthem. For him the song was not set in stone, immutable the day it was recorded for Warner Brothers. It continued to evolve as it had in the beginning. As new events occurred that captured his imagination, he wove them into his ever-growing anthem. In the 1970s, at President Carter's inauguration, another series of events transpired that clicked flawlessly into place in the narrative and created a new punch line for the story.

Arlo was invited to the 1976 inaugural ball. There he ran into Chip

Carter, the president's son, who had been looking all over for the folksinger because he had to tell him about an amazing discovery. While moving into the White House, Chip had come across Richard Nixon's record library, which included, much to his surprise, a copy of "Alice's Restaurant." (Of course, it would have been more surprising if he had uncovered a copy of "Presidential Rag," which skewered Nixon with such lines as "You're the one we voted for / so you must take the blame / for handing out authority / to men who are insane.") While Arlo was amused by this little factoid, it would be some time before another fact would cross his mind. One day, probably when he was having a chuckle at the thought of Nixon singing a bar of "Alice's Restaurant," he remembered Watergate, the infamous White House tapes, and their even more infamous eighteen-minute, twenty-second gap — the exact length of "Alice's Restaurant." It was not only a great coincidence and a great story, it fit in perfectly with the structure of the song. "I asked myself, Arlo, how many things in this world are exactly eighteen minutes twenty seconds long?" he says to hearty laughter.

So for a long time he knew he would record an "Alice" update someday. As early as 1988 Sharon Palma told a *Berkshire Eagle* reporter that he would rerecord Alice "hopefully soon, but with him you never can tell."

When he found himself back in the old church, everything seemed to fall into place. He could record an update of the song in the very building in which the infamous Thanksgiving dinner had taken place and celebrate the event (it was actually recorded three times over three days) as a fund-raiser for his new nonprofit organization.

Because of the perennial popularity of "Alice's Restaurant," Warner Brothers had not released the album rights to Rising Son Records. Warner owned the recordings, but Arlo owned the compositions. If he were to record the songs afresh he could release them on his own label. While he was revisiting his past, the old church, and "Alice's Restaurant," he decided to go ahead and produce a full-fledged musical revisit. The album would be redone in its entirety, with all the same songs in the same sequence as in the original. Even the album cover was faithfully restaged. Arlo, now thirty years older, sat at a table wielding a fork and knife and wearing only a napkin tucked into a nonexistent shirt. Arlo says the napkin was suspended by a "top-secret" method, which this author suspects was cellophane tape. In the updated version, Arlo decided against wearing the bowler hat he had sported in the original because, he said, he "gave up bowling." The other major difference in the packaging was that the new version was released on compact disc, which eliminated the curious sight of a single song taking up an entire side of a vinyl album.

When the revised version of "Alice" was released on Rising Son Records with a limited distribution network, it initially shipped primarily to military bases, Arlo told a *Berkshire Eagle* reporter. "It's the most terrific, funniest, wonderful reminder of what the song is all about, which is that in the face of great turmoil, you have to maintain your sense of humor."

Arlo, Sarah, and Abe Guthrie in concert.

A new Thanksgiving tradition seems to have taken hold at the Guthrie Center as well. For the past few years in October, Arlo has held a pre-Thanksgiving concert, which has been recorded for syndicated radio airplay on Thanksgiving Day. As with many of his shows, the concerts have become family affairs. For several years Arlo has been accompanied by his son Abe, who plays keyboard and acts as stage manager and sound manager. Recently daughter Sarah has joined the family business. She sings and plays the guitar with her father and brother for a few numbers. Daughter Annie is instrumental in running things behind the scenes at Rising Son Records, and Abe's wife Lisa has recently taken over management of the Guthrie Center.

AMY FELD

Replacing a window with a door: Henry Kirchdorfer III with Lee Palma (standing).

Almost simultaneously with the release of the new "Alice's Restaurant," Arlo released "Mystic Journey," which, as the title suggests, is inspired largely by his spiritual studies. Together, the albums seem to sum up what the Guthrie Center is about: spiritual exploration and a new way of looking at an old time.

More recently, some renovations on the center have been completed. So far, much of it has involved replacing windows with doors and doors with windows. Eventually Arlo would like to take out the "maze of rooms" and restore it as close to its original condition as possible. In the summer of 1998 the peeling paint was covered with white siding. Mary Sachs was so pleased to see the face-lift that she sent Arlo a letter and thanked him on behalf of all the former church members, who, she said, would be pleased to see it looking so much nicer than it had.

Shortly thereafter, Rising Son Records moved out of the church and into the former Kresgee building in Pittsfield, Massachusetts. The church is now home only to the Guthrie Center and Foundation.

"People were confused," Arlo says. "They couldn't understand why they had to contribute to a record company. It's easier just to move the thing out of there than trying to explain why it's easier for us to be in there. But we outgrew it, anyway. We had too much stuff going on, too much business going on, and it was losing its ability to respond to people on a personal basis, people who wanted to spend some quiet time there. I didn't mean for it to happen so soon, but then one day mysteriously about a week before Christmas, all the phones in the church blew out just after we'd sent out tens of thousands of catalogs with the church phone number — call us and place an order. All of a sudden there were no phones and people were calling. We were late sending out the catalog anyway, and everyone that wanted stuff was calling and no one was getting through. It was easier for us to put in a whole new phone system in the Kresgee building, where there'd never been a phone, than it was to restore the phones at the church because it was so antiquated. Since we'd have to move out a year later we took all the stuff and moved it. Eventually we'll have our [music] venues here, and the church will be just the church. There will be events there from time to time, but for the most part it will be entirely and singularly what it was meant to be."

Events like the rerecording of "Alice" were special, but to Arlo, what makes the church really meaningful is that it is meaningful to other people for a variety of reasons. There are the members of the community who come out of curiosity or because they've heard good things are going to happen there. There are the fans who come to see the setting of *Alice's Restaurant.* Today the Guthrie Center has more members (people who send in $25 once a year and receive the newsletter) than it ever had as a church. Some, members of the Berkshire community, are active volunteers. Some live nearby and come to visit from time to time, happy that it is available to them if they want to meditate, pray, take advantage of programs, or reminisce about the good old days. Sometimes people sit at the altar and leave mementos behind — lockets, stones, angels, and so on.

Yet the locals are only part of the greater Guthrie Center community. Thanks to the Internet, a new kind of community has sprung up, made up of people who talk to one another every day across state and national boundaries. Some who consider themselves members of the center live as far away as Australia and have never actually been inside it.

Until the Internet came along, most people who appreciated Arlo's music were largely unaware of the other people out there who also enjoyed it. Once they did meet on line, they discovered they had many other things in common and developed their own set of in-jokes and repartee on computer message boards. This fledgling on-line community was given a boost about five years ago when Jackie Guthrie discovered an active Arlo Guthrie discussion group on Prodigy and another on America on Line. She talked with the fans and convinced her husband to log on as well. He enjoyed reading what the fans were saying "behind his back" as well as the reaction he received when he answered ques-

Tom Paxton (left) and Arlo playing on the porch of the Guthrie Center.

JUDY BEISLER

tions or, more commonly, posted a cryptic message and then disappeared from view for days or weeks.

Shortly thereafter, Dave Downin, an electronics technician from Laurel, Maryland, was designing his own Web page. He didn't want it to be an average listing of hobbies and photographs of pets. As he put it, "I didn't want to do anything lame. Whenever I would search for Web pages about Arlo, nothing would appear. I figured there must be other Arlo fans out there, so I thought that kind of page might actually be useful to someone."

Around this time Dave attended an Arlo Guthrie concert in Alexandria, Virginia. During the performance, Arlo mentioned reading a message someone had left on a Prodigy message board. Dave went home, ordered a Prodigy start-up disc, and found the musician's e-mail address. He sent Arlo a short message telling him about his Web page. "I had absolutely no idea at the time that I would get to know Arlo, or that he would ever know my name or who I was," he says.

Although Dave admits that the prototype of "Arlonet" was not particularly impressive compared to what it has become, Arlo was thrilled with it.

"I think he said, 'Wow,'" Dave recalls.

Arlo made an appointment with Dave to discuss his ideas for the Web page. "He said that he had looked at Jerry Jeff Walker's Web page,"

Dave says. "And it had a thing on it that counted how many people had visited the site. He wanted to know if I could do something like that for his page."

Over the next few months, Arlonet was transformed from a fan's tribute to an official Arlo Guthrie Web presence. Dave now works with the Rising Son Records office, posting concert dates, news, and the Arlo Guthrie catalog. He also maintains a Web page for the Guthrie Center. While it may have become "official," Arlonet is still almost entirely the product of Downin's ideas and work. "I think the counter was pretty much Arlo's only contribution," he says with a laugh.

The site has earned multiple awards, including The Point's "Top 5% of All Web Pages." It has also made Arlo Guthrie a fan of Dave Downin.

"One time I was at a concert with my parents," Dave recalls, "and Arlo pointed right at me. He said, 'That's the man responsible for our Web page. It's all Dave Downin's fault.' I couldn't believe he did that."

Along with Arlonet, Dave set up an Internet newsgroup, alt.music.guthrie, and a Web-based chat room called Blunderchat, or "Blat" to those who prefer abbreviations. The newsgroup is devoted to both Arlo and Woody. Because the two musicians have distinctly different audiences, the newsgroup has created an odd cohabitation. Woody Guthrie fans occasionally come in search of information, looking for vintage recordings, but they have generally been overshadowed, and perhaps a little overwhelmed, by the "Blunderites."

Like most fan newsgroups, alt.music.guthrie is more of a social club than a discussion of the artist's work. The fans sometimes go for weeks without ever typing the name "Arlo" or even anything remotely comprehensible to the uninitiated. A person logging into the newsgroup to find information about Arlo's latest CD is more likely to find a guide to "Blunderite vocabulary," a rambling, disjointed series of song lyrics, or one-liners about "mooses" (an allusion to Arlo's book for children, *Mooses Come Walking*).

When the conversation does turn to the musician, it is as likely to be about his personality, charm, and physical traits as about his music.

"Naturally, I thought that someone would be saying something that had to do with me," says Arlo of the newsgroup. "I'm amazed how little I'm a part of it. It's great to see so many people enjoying their own lives so much."

"The best thing about Arlonet is all the people I have gotten to know," Dave says. "I used to go to a concert with a friend or two. Now when I go, there are all kinds of people who know me. I have made some wonderful friends . . . It's all Arlo Guthrie's fault."

Arlo's own interest in the Internet fueled his desire to create the children's cyber center and other computer-based learning programs in the church. When he goes on tour, he carries a Macintosh laptop with him. He is such a Mac fan that he sometimes says he would like to replace the one missing piece of stained glass in the church's rose window with a Macintosh apple. He once even managed to get in a plug for his computer of choice during a brief Thanksgiving appearance on MSNBC (a collaboration between NBC and Microsoft).

"Who would have thought!" Arlo laughs. "I wish some of my friends who have gone were here to see the stuff that is going on today. They would love it! I love the idea of people all over the world being able to freely communicate with each other."

While he enjoys the opportunity to meet with his most devoted fans, Arlo has learned that the feedback he gets from them may not always be useful. When Blunderites began posting their "Top 10 Favorite Arlo Songs," Arlo got to work changing his concert set list, only to find that the majority of the people who come to his shows want to hear the old favorites like "City of New Orleans," and not the somewhat obscure selections that the other fans favor.

"It's a whole different crowd than the one that hangs around on the Blunder-Boards," Arlo wrote in the *Rolling Blunder Review*. "New people want to hear the old stuff. The Blunderites are tired of that stuff."

What they rarely tire of is each other. They call the Guthrie Center simply "the church," and they use the occasional concerts and events that take place there as an excuse to meet in a central location. They sometimes talk about such journeys as "a pilgrimage." The church is now the home of a community that otherwise has no geographical base at all.

Lisa Jackson, a Blunderchat regular and Guthrie Center member from Texas, visited the church for the first time a year ago. "I was in awe of it," she says. "It's a beautiful old building, and it has so much history. There's a warmth about it when you think about what Arlo stands for. He has been given this legacy from his parents. They gave him this legacy that we weren't just put on this earth to do for ourselves. That's a message that you see in his music all throughout the years, even when he was a young man. He's not preachy, but he has a way of making us see we do need to extend a hand. I don't know anything about what Ma is teaching. I'm a Christian. I recognize that there are other religions out there and everyone has to choose their own path. That doesn't take away from the whole message of the Guthrie Center anyway, that we all have souls and we're all spiritual beings and we all have to find our own way of making sense of it. Arlo is the biggest draw, what he represents and that I was there with friends, meeting people I'd met on line."

Sherry Boullt believes the church could be located anywhere and still mean as much to the fans. "It's not your average community," she says. "The people who really experienced it [in the 1960s] are what breathed the life into it. It has that mystique of hippiedom and walking in the rain. We look at it almost as this haven."

That is why it was important to Arlo to buy the place back and make it available to his friends and fans. "I wanted to provide a place for them and a history for them, for all of us," he says. "Especially those of us who came out of the '60s, who were reinterpreting what spirituality is all about, reinterpreting what religious tradition is all about, making it less of an exclusive club that we belong to and making it more of a practical challenge of how do we get through with life. That's the big question that all of the religions try to address. The question still is there for everybody. Those questions are what we commonly refer to as spirituality, that innate part of ourselves that we don't know if it's part of us. We don't know if it will go on after us. We don't know where it came from to begin with. We don't know much about it. The older you get, the more you think of it, because you realize the part of you you're familiar with is disappearing on you. And these questions become really important to young people and little kids who are dealing with life-and-death stuff. And it's important to people who through no apparent reason got the shit beat out of them by parents who were more interested in getting stoned. For all those people, we've set aside a place for them to think about those things."

Although Arlo stresses the fact that the Guthrie Center is not a religion, he does provide space for spiritual discussion and on occasion has had the pleasure of performing marriage ceremonies, which his religious training legally allows him to do. For the most part, he says, his church duties are far more mundane, like sweeping the sanctuary or changing the light bulbs.

"I don't provide the answers to anybody. It's not my thing," he says. "What I do like to provide is the space to discuss and share what we've discovered. To me, the memories are the people. Madeline, the woman who called us up one time crying because her husband was in the hospital and the free rides provided for the elderly came by at seven in the morning but visiting hours weren't until ten, so she was spending all her heating money on taxis. She said, 'I'm calling you because there is no one else who can do anything. They said you work with people with AIDS, but I just need a ride.' So we formed a group of people who took Madeline every day to see her husband. Eventually she hung out at the church every day. She had the best jokes, smart wit, incredible wit, so funny. She's gone now.

"It's the people that are the memories. Some of the kids that have been in there and some of the art that some of them have done. The moments are made by the people themselves. I have at times wondered whether all this was worth it or not. Every time another one of these faces smiles in the midst of all that — when I look back on all the people we've made friends with whose memories are now part of the church — it was worth it if just one of them found some kindred spirits in there.

"These were not people who shared my sense of spirituality or education or anything like that. These were just people who liked what I liked, and the people I liked, or liked me. Not one of them took a course or sat down and did meditation. These people brought their own thing. I knew that when they came on their own, doing their own thing, that I was absolutely vindicated for not coming in with another 'Arlo's plan to save the world.' The world didn't need that. Frankly, mine keeps getting revised anyway. I haven't finished it yet. Maybe it's just a way to occupy my mind when there's nothing good on TV.

"All these people have just become friends. I married one friend of mine and his wife, so I did one full circle with somebody, married them and buried them also. That's part of the responsibility that I have there more in a traditional sense, part of my responsibility for those people. To those people for whom I can provide some kind of service, it's perfect. That's the stuff that nobody knows about. It's the things you can't really tell. It's not part of a history so much. All those people who participated in a building, who came in there when they were young, who spent some time there, who lived there — most of them are gone now. But now I think it's nice for them to know — I don't know if they do, maybe they don't — but it's nice for them to know that that building has become important to other people as it was for them at some point, and it provides for some of the same type of heartfelt compassion and understanding that I hope was happening for them. And if not, well, it's happening now. It's not being provided by me necessarily, but it's provided by people who are drawn by a certain magnetism, and the more they take care of each other, the better job I'm doing."

ED HYMAN, AUTOPHOTOS

Arlo shows Eveline Burgert's memorial plaque to guests.

"If society has deconsecrated the church, can an alternative community reconsecrate it?"

— Venable Herndon

Epilogue

The screenplay for *Alice's Restaurant* set out to answer the question "If society has deconsecrated the church, can an alternative community reconsecrate it?" Although Venable Herndon said the answer in the movie was no, even he is not certain that was the right answer. Is the deconsecrated church in Van Deusenville a holy place? Was it a holy place when Alice and Ray lived there? Was it holy when Roland Ginzel and Ellen Lanyon were creating art in its sanctuary? Is it holy now, as the Guthrie Center? Has it ever, in fact, stopped being holy?

At the end of the film *Alice's Restaurant*, the viewer is left with an empty feeling. The dream of a new community had failed. Assuming that this interpretation is accurate — if the friends who spent time at the building in the 1960s had a dream of a new kind of church community and it failed — would that mean the answer to the question of reconsecration is no? For that to be the case, only that which is *permanent* could be considered holy. Trinity Church itself, because it didn't last, would also have to be considered a failure and not sacred. One need only speak briefly to Mary Sachs to know this was not true.

Trinity Church, in all its brevity, was the place where the children of Van Deusenville were baptized, where they married, and where their children came to mourn their passing. In both its architecture and the theology, it was a testament to the transitory and holy. The architecture, with its symbolic representation of Noah's Ark and of redemption through the crucifixion of Christ, demonstrates that the world is one of constant death and rebirth, destruction and renewal, and that this process itself is holy.

The Episcopal Church came into existence when Henry VIII officially broke ties with the Catholic Church, yet retained many of its traditions. When the colonists revolted against England to carve out an independent nation, that church, minus an oath of loyalty to the Crown, remained. The architecture of Trinity Church is also a symbol of this process of creating new traditions from the old. Architect Richard Upjohn adapted the designs of grand medieval churches for their new settings in rural America.

When another revolution of sorts rocked the church in Van Deusenville and transformed it from a place of worship to a private home frequented by forward-thinking young people, it might have appeared that tradition was no longer revered, but in fact these young people based their new way of life on what had come before. Even in the most rebellious times, people hold on to certain aspects of tradition. It is no coincidence that in the 1960s young musical artists scored radio hits with old folk songs, melodies borrowed from Bach, and lyrics from Ecclesiastes. Arlo Guthrie's own musical career could be said to be a lot like his church: It was built on the foundations of what had come before — the music of his father and his contemporaries — and yet it was something brand-new, built to suit the needs of a new generation.

In fact, all artistic accomplishment may result from an artist's willingness to break with tradition and at the same time revere certain aspects of that tradition.

"It is difficult to see how a person can be creative without being both traditional and conservative and at the same time rebellious and iconoclastic," wrote Mihaly Csikszentmikalyi in his book *Creativity*. "Being only traditional leaves the domain unchanged; constantly taking chances without regard to what has been valued in the past rarely leads to novelty that is accepted as an improvement."

The Guthrie Center today draws on its past. Memories of its *Alice's Restaurant* days bring people to the doors. Those people may form a new and viable community that honors what has passed as it looks to the future. But the question remains: Is it a holy place? What must take place before we can consider a building holy?

The answer may lie in the word "holy" itself, which dates back to pre-Christian times. It is related to the words "holistic" and "whole" and means that which is inviolate, intact, complete. To feel holy is therefore to feel whole. By that definition, anytime someone sits anywhere and feels whole — however briefly — he is on sacred ground.

It was holy when they laid the cornerstone for Trinity Church in 1830. It was holy when Samuel Parker gave sermons that inspired people to help the less fortunate in the community. It was holy when Mary Sachs's sister taught Sunday School. It was holy when the bell rang out to announce the end of the war. It was holy when friends sang together and felt understood and loved. It was holy when people danced in the sanctuary. It was holy when children who'd had tough lives came and played music and ate cookies that tasted good. Anytime a person steps into the old church building and the problems of the world seem to be lifted, if only for a moment, the building is consecrated.

"I feel more connected to God there than in any other building," says Sherry Boullt. "My connection to it isn't as a church. It's more of a spiritual place than a religious place. When I'm there with my friends, we're all on our own path and we can all be there together."

Arlo Guthrie says he loves the place. He probably expressed that love best in a recent issue of the *Rolling Blunder Review:*

> I miss the days I spent in the church a few years ago when
> I was there almost every day. In the summer evenings when
> the sun was going down, what Ma calls cowdust time, I would
> light the candles and the incense and sit quietly in my prayer
> and meditation. Occasionally someone would come in and
> silently witness the rich stillness . . . the air thick with
> shakti . . . living, for a little while each day, beyond everyday

reality somewhere close to the truth. Just being aware of the sacredness of the breath we share. The breath of this generation is beginning to return from where it comes. And although it may be decades before it is extinguished completely, the finality of this borrowed breath is beginning to become an everyday reality for many friends. People confront these thoughts differently. Many seek comfort in a life after life; a continuation of self in another or different dimension. Some become even more immersed and attached to the very life they know will end. Others become chemically oblivious through a variety of self-prescribed solutions. Frankly, I'm just waiting to see what happens next. Come as whoever you are. Seek your life — become immersed. No one will judge you here. Leave your judgment, ambition and chemicals just outside the door. You can pick them up on the way out. Come see what happens next! Someday, maybe I'll have these moments to enjoy again. Meanwhile, I give them to whoever finds them valuable. The incense is there. The candles are there. The sun goes down every day.

The nonprofit organizations, the Guthrie Center and Foundation, are just getting started. Whether they live up to their potential is yet to be seen — how many people will come, what they will do, whom they will serve, how long it will continue. But in the present time the doors will be open, and everyone is welcome to bring their own god and make the moments holy.

Bibliography

Albany (NY) Times Union. Various articles.

Anderson, Christy Jo. "St. Paul's Church, Stockbridge, Massachusetts: The History of a Church and the Decorative Arts." Paper written for Dr. Paul F. Norton, University of Massachusetts, 1982.

"Arlo Guthrie." *The New Yorker*, 6 January 1968.

Benson, Arnold. "Night Alice, Night Obie." *New England Monthly*, January 1986.

Berkshire Courier, Great Barrington, MA. Various articles.

Berkshire Eagle, Pittsfield, MA. Various articles.

Berkshire Family History Association. Archives. Berkshire Athenaeum. Pittsfield, MA.

Berkshire Historical and Scientific Society. *Collections of the Berkshire Historical and Scientific Society*. Pittsfield, MA, 1894.

Bernstein, Phyllis. "Staunch Stockbridge Makes the Scene." *Springfield Sunday Republican*, 21 September 1969.

Biedermann, Hans. *Dictionary of Symbolism: Cultural Icons and the Meanings Behind Them*. New York: Meridian, 1994.

Biskind, Peter. *Easy Riders, Raging Bulls: How the Sex-Drugs-and-Rock 'n' Roll Generation Saved Hollywood*. New York: Touchstone, 1998.

Blasi, Ralph. "Dede Allen — The Force on the Cutting Room Floor." *Show: The Magazine of Films and the Arts*, January 1970.

Bosworth, Patricia. "Arlo's Still Searching." *Sunday Herald Traveler Magazine*, 19 October 1969.

Boullt, Sherry. Telephone interview by author. 10 February 1999.

Braun, Saul. "Alice and Ray and Yesterday's Flowers." *Playboy*, October 1969.

Brock, Alice May. Interview by author. Provincetown, MA, 17 February 1999.

———. *Alice's Restaurant Cookbook*. New York: Random House, 1969.

———. *My Life as a Restaurant*. Woodstock, NY: Overlook Press, 1975.

Casey, Partick. "Arlo Guthrie Embraces Internet as 'Last Bastion of Real Freedom.'" Associated Press, 17 September 1998.

Chapman, Gerard. *St. James Parish, Great Barrington, Massachusetts, 1762–1962*. North Conway, NH: The Reporter Press, 1962.

_____. *St. Paul's Episcopal Parish, Stockbridge, Massachusetts, 1834–1984.* Stockbridge, MA: St. Paul's Protestant Episcopal Parish, 1985.

Child, Hamilton. *Gazetteer of Berkshire County, MA, 1725–1885. 1885.* Syracuse, New York: Hamilton Child, 1885.

Cowie, Peter, ed. *International Film Guide 1969.* London: Tantivy Press, 1969.

Cronkite, Kathy. *On the Edge of the Spotlight.* New York: William Morrow and Company, 1981.

Crowdus, Gary, and Richard Porton. "The Importance of a Singular, Guiding Vision: An Interview with Arthur Penn." *Cineaste,* 1 January 1994.

Dass, Ram, and Mirabai Bush. *Compassion in Action.* New York: Bell Tower, 1992.

Deitz, Roger. "The Rising Son." *Acoustic Guitar Magazine,* September 1998.

Denucci, Debra. AOL Instant Message interview by author. 11 February 1999.

DiMartino, Dave. *Singer-Songwriters.* New York: Billboard Books, 1994.

Downin, David. Telephone interview by author. September 1997.

Dreifus, Claudia. "Arlo Guthrie." *The Progressive,* February 1993.

Drumm, Pam. Interview by author. Great Barrington, MA, 1 March 1999.

Elliot, Steve. Telephone interview by author. 28 February 1999.

Episcopal Diocese of Western Massachusetts. Records of Trinity Church.

Fass, Bob. Telephone interview by author. 18 May 1999.

Pittsfield (MA) Journal, 26 March 1915.

Florence, Suzanne. Interview by author. Great Barrington, MA, 5 December 1998.

Friedman, Benno. Telephone interview by author. 14 March 1999.

Gable, John Allen. *The Goodness That Doth Crown Our Days: A History of Trinity Parish Lenox, Massachusetts.* North Adams, MA: Trinity Parish Lenox, 1993.

Garcia, Bob. "The New Guthrie: Arlo." *Underground Digest: The Best of the Underground Press.* March 1967.

Geisel, Ellen. "Arlo Guthrie: The Story of Reuben Clamzo." *Dirty Linen,* April/May 1992.

Gelatt, Roland. "SR Goes to the Movies: Arlo as Arlo." *Saturday Review,* 20 August 1969.

Ginzel, Roland, and Ellen Lanyon. Interview by author. Stockbridge, MA, 28 February 1999.

Giuliano, Charles. "The Stockbridge Scene." *Sunday Herald Traveler Magazine,* 19 October 1969.

Guthrie, Arlo. Interview by author. Pittsfield, MA, 13 April 1999.

_____. *Alice's Restaurant.* Ryko, 1998. Official soundtrack.

_____, ed. *Rolling Blunder Review.* Various issues.

Guthrie, Arlo, and Cable Neuhaus. "Coping: Despite the Shadow of His Father's (and Possibly His Own) Deadly Disease, a Folk Hero Celebrates Life." *People,* 7 September 1987.

Hall, Russell. "Arlo Guthrie Revisits Alice." *Y'All On-Line Magazine,* www.accessatlanta.com.

Harwood, Diana. Interview by author. Housatonic, MA, 28 January 1999.

Hebner, Tom and Frances. Recorded interview by Rachel Fletcher. 29 September 1988.

Hedgepeth, William. "The Successful Anarchist." *Look,* 4 February 1969.

Herndon, Venable. Telephone interview by author. 18 May 1999.

Herndon, Venable, and Arthur Penn. *Alice's Restaurant*. New York: Doubleday and Company, 1970. Screenplay.

History of the County of Berkshire Massachusetts in Two Parts. The First Being a General View of the County, The Second, an Account of the Several Towns by Gentlemen in the County, Clergymen and Laymen. Pittsfield, MA: Samuel W. Bush, Printer, 1829.

History of Berkshire County Massachusetts, with Biographical Sketches of Prominent Men. Vol. 2. New York: J. B. Beers and Company, 1885.

Hoffman, Ellen. "Alice's Life Without the Restaurant." *Washington Post*, 4 September 1970.

Jackson, Lisa. Telephone interview by author. 10 May 1999.

Klein, Joe. *Woody Guthrie: A Life*. New York: Alfred A. Knopf, 1980.

_____. "Notes on a Native Son." *Rolling Stone*, 10 March 1997.

Kleinwald, Paul. Telephone interview by author. 11 March 1999.

Koch, John. "Arlo Guthrie: The Interview." *Boston Globe*, 18 January 1998.

Lansky, Aaron. "A Tribute to Courage: Marjorie Guthrie Remembered." *The Book Peddler*, Newsletter of the National Yiddish Book Center, Winter 1984.

Lawrence, Arthur. *Historic Record of St. Paul's Episcopal Church, Stockbridge, MA*. Berkshire County Historical Society, 1905.

"Letters to the Editor." *Life*, 18 April 1969.

Lewis, Joseph Ward. *Berkshire Men of Worth*. Vol 4. July 12, 1939–Aug 13, 1941. Berkshire Athenaeum. Pittsfield, MA.

Mannuzza, Vivi. "Alice's Restaurant Revisited — 20 Years Later." *Berkshire Record*, 7 February 1992.

Middleton, Pierce. Telephone interview by author. 1 March 1999.

Morganstern, Joseph, and Stefan Kanfer, eds. *Film 69/70*. New York: Simon and Schuster, 1970.

"On the Road . . . But Not With Alice." *Berkshire Record*, 3 August 1990.

Orteza, Arsenio. "Arlo and Ma." *Christian Century*, 5 May 1993.

Outlaw, Geoff. Telephone interview by author. 25 May 1999.

Palma, Sharon. Interview by author. Great Barrington, MA, 15 April 1999.

Pelkey, Mary. Telephone interview by author. 5 March 1999.

Penn, Arthur. Telephone interview by author. 20 July 1999.

Ponder, Bo. "I Just Look Like Any Other Freak." *TV and Movie Screen*, March 1970.

Powell, Joanna. *Things I Should Have Said to My Father*. New York: Avon, 1994.

Report of the Proceedings of the First International Conference on the Challenge of Underused Church Property and the Search for Alternatives. Cambridge, MA: The Cheswick Center, 1975.

Robbins, Rick. Interview by author. Housatonic, MA, 24 February 1999.

Rogovoy, Seth. "Arlo Guthrie Offers a Menu of Music and Politics." *Berkshires Weekly*, 3 July 1992.

Rose, Frank. "At Home with Arlo." *Zoo World*, 4 July 1974.

Sachs, Mary. Interview by author. Great Barrington, MA, 28 January and 6 March 1999.

Sahler, Louis Hasbrouck. *The History and Genealogy of the Van Deusens of Van Deusen Manor, Great Barrington, Berkshire County*. Great Barrington, MA: Berkshire Courier Company, n.d.

Salisbury Association. *Historical Collections Relating to the Town of Salisbury*. Vol. 1. Salisbury, CT, 1913.

Sandahl, Linda J. *Rock Films*. New York: Facts on File Publications, 1987.

Stickney, John. "Alice's Family of Folk Song Fame Becomes a Movie." *Life*, 28 March 1969.

Taylor, Charles J. *History of Great Barrington, Mass*. With extension to 1922 by George Edwin MacLean. Great Barrington, MA: Berkshire Courier, 1928.

This Is the Arlo Guthrie Book. New York: Amsco Music Publishing Company, 1969.

United Artists. *Alice's Restaurant*. Pressbook. 1969.

Van Deusen, Albert H. *Van Deusen Family*. New York: Frank Allaben Genealogical Co., n.d.

Whitman, Cannon Robert S. S. Telephone interview by author. 12 April 1999.

Woliver, Robbie. *Hoot! A 25-Year History of the Greenwich Village Music Scene*. New York: St. Martin's Press, 1986.

Wood, Robin. *Arthur Penn*. New York: Praeger, 1970.

Zimmerman, Paul D. "Alice's Restaurant's Kids." *Newsweek*, 29 September 1969.

Zito, Tom. "Alice's Revisited: A Taste of Mussels and the Establishment." *Washington Post*, 3 March 1974.

Index